Ecosystem-Led Growth

A Blueprint for Sales and Marketing Success Using the Power of Partnerships

Bob Moore

WILEY

Published by John Wiley & Sons, Inc., Hoboken, New Jersey.
Published simultaneously in Canada.

For general information on our other products and services or for technical support, please contact our Customer Care Department within the United States at (800) 762-2974, outside the United States at (317) 572-3993 or fax (317) 572-4002.

Wiley also publishes its books in a variety of electronic formats. Some content that appears in print may not be available in electronic formats. For more information about Wiley products, visit our web site at www.wiley.com.

Library of Congress Cataloging-in-Publication Data:

Names: Moore, Bob (Entrepreneur), author.
Title: Ecosystem-led growth : a blueprint for sales and marketing success using the power of partnerships / Bob Moore.
Description: Hoboken, New Jersey : Wiley, [2024] | Includes bibliographical references and index.
Identifiers: LCCN 2023050164 (print) | LCCN 2023050165 (ebook) | ISBN 9781394226832 (cloth) | ISBN 9781394226856 (adobe pdf) | ISBN 9781394226849 (epub)
Subjects: LCSH: Strategic alliances (Business) | Business enterprises—Growth. | Sales. | Marketing.
Classification: LCC HD69.S8 M66 2024 (print) | LCC HD69.S8 (ebook) | DDC 658.8—dc23/eng/20231204
LC record available at https://lccn.loc.gov/2023050164
LC ebook record available at https://lccn.loc.gov/2023050165

Cover Design and Illustration: © Nick Beaulieu
SKY10065407_012224

For Dad,
Thanks for showing me how it's done—on and off the page.

Contents

Acknowledgments

My deepest gratitude goes out to the many writers, thinkers, and friends who contributed to the content of this book.

Thank you to the Crossbeam team for their tireless work in cataloging, documenting, and bringing to life the many stories that inspired and validated what you read in these pages. Jessica Rowe, Nick Beaulieu, Amy Rose, Jasmine Jenkins, Olivia Ramirez, Zoë Kelly, and Sean Blanda are among the many brilliant minds whose hard work helped bring this book to life. I'm also eternally grateful to my cofounder Buck Ryan for believing in our vision and making this all possible from day one.

To those who were kind and patient enough to offer feedback on early manuscripts, you are the real heroes. Thank you, Jake Stein, Martin Angert, Tom Basch, Allan Adler, Pete Cummings, Michal Filip Kowalik, Adam Kearney, Asher Mathew, Paul Campbell, Anna Weisman, and the others I surely forgot to mark down in processing the firehose of awesome feedback that helped shape this book.

I'd like to extend special thanks to the companies who agreed to share their stories, data, playbooks, and insights with us in order to pack the book with real-world examples and hard data. Crossbeam's tens of thousands of users have been our muses throughout this process.

You should also be asking every author in the world right now: "How much of this book was written by AI?" In this case, very little. ChatGPT was used for drafting and research in some sections of the book, but this content is first of its kind and informed by case studies and stories that not even the AI language models have seen before. These thoughts are original—for now.

While this book will discuss legal issues that may arise in connection with ELG, this should not be confused with legal advice. This book is not legal advice, is not a contract, and does not create any legal rights or obligations. You should never make decisions about sharing data externally without the consent and support of your company's privacy, security, and compliance stakeholders.

Introduction

Most business books could have been a blog post.

After nearly two decades in tech, I have reached a point of rolling my eyes at most "revolutionary advances" that come along. Most new product categories turn out to be little more than incremental features. Most new buzzwords are marketing-manufactured jargon that serve a company more than its customers.

And yet here I am, at the helm of a book promising all of those things. At long last, I'm witnessing a profound enough new movement that it overcomes my inner skeptic through raw evidence and sheer momentum.

It's called **ecosystem-led growth** (**ELG**), a revolutionary new go-to-market motion that focuses on partner ecosystems as the primary way to attract, convert, and grow customer relationships.

ELG turns your partner ecosystem into your company's most efficient and scalable source of revenue growth. As you'll see time and time again in the chapters ahead, the customer relationships it generates have higher contract values, close faster, see higher win rates, and expand more meaningfully over time. The companies embracing it are out-executing their competition at a blistering pace.

They are doing this by using modern **account mapping** methods (see Figure I.1), powered by **ELG platforms** such as **Crossbeam**, to unlock a powerful new data layer made up of intelligence, context, and next best actions from across your partner ecosystem.

This new wellspring of partner data and influence ripples into every stage of their revenue funnels:

- You'll learn how **ecosystem-led marketing** is changing the way Stripe executives think about their funnel using ecosystem-qualified leads,

1

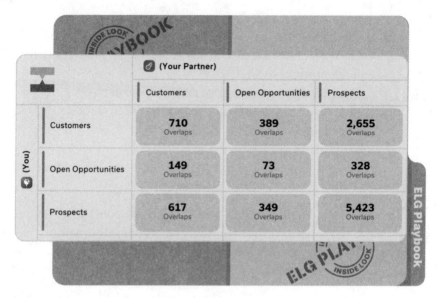

The following is within the figure:

(Your Partner)	Customers	Open Opportunities	Prospects
Customers	710 Overlaps	389 Overlaps	2,655 Overlaps
Open Opportunities	149 Overlaps	73 Overlaps	328 Overlaps
Prospects	617 Overlaps	349 Overlaps	5,423 Overlaps

FIGURE I.1 The account mapping matrix.

Gainsight designs customer events by building curated audiences, and Okta Ventures moves the needle for its portfolio with qualified introductions (including a playbook that increased partner-influenced revenue from 3% to 80% of a company's new business in a single year).

- You'll get an inside look at how Braze, Fivetran, and many others have built an **ecosystem-led sales** motion inside of their revenue teams that use proprietary ecosystem intelligence, personalization, and co-selling playbooks to increase contract values, win at higher rates, and speed up deal cycles (including playbooks that have increased one company's close rates by 40%, grown its pipeline by 44%, and increased its average deal size by 50%).

- You'll see how innovators such as RollWorks and Bombora have systematically infused **ecosystem-led customer success** to key parts of their post-sale customer experience, reducing churn and expanding revenue per account over time (including a playbook that decreased churn rates by 3.5x).

- You'll learn how Gong, Intercom, and others have rolled out ELG playbooks to create a virtuous cycle of **ecosystem development.** These playbooks will show you how to prioritize partners, invest resources intelligently, and grow flourishing ecosystems at low cost and with lean teams.

The resulting map of ecosystem-led growth playbooks (see Figure I.2) will be our handy guide as we walk down your funnel, passing through your ecosystem at every step as it accrues even more scale and value to feed back into your company's growth.

The raw ingredients here are not new: partnerships, data, people, focus, and grit. What's new is the technology that pulls them together and the market moment that makes their potential so clear.

This book is being printed at a turbulent moment in economic history. In the early part of this decade, cheap capital and low interest rates from the pandemic era drove a bubble in the valuations (and burn rates) of growth-stage technology companies.

Just as rapidly, those valuations came crashing down, and those same companies were forced to quickly refocus on efficiency. The ensuing whip-lash has led to the demise of many once-promising companies and made new superstars out of those that cracked the code of efficient growth. For most, however, unanswered questions about the best paths forward still remain.

Meanwhile, advances in artificial intelligence are undermining the strategies of old, making traditional growth playbooks commoditized at best and obsolete at worst. Add in the most complex regulatory, privacy, and security environment ever seen, and you have a market that will punish those who cannot adapt quickly.

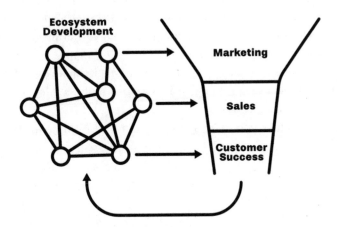

FIGURE I.2   The ELG playbook map.

So what happens when the **return on investment (ROI)** on every growth playbook goes upside down, yet the market demands lean and profitable growth? You get a once-in-a-career market moment where only the strong will survive and the definition of every "best practice" for growing an enduring company will be rewritten.

Companies must now discover new avenues of growth that are proprietary to them and unable to be commoditized. These strategies must scale without a ceiling along with the company's long-term trajectory. And they must be lean and efficient in how they deliver their results.

These new growth playbooks must be ecosystem-led.

In the chapters that follow, we'll dive into the origin of the ELG movement, the technology that paved the way, the market dynamics that make it so compelling, and the play-by-play instructions for bringing ELG to life inside your organization.

You'll learn about how shifting paradigms of artificial intelligence, regulation, and data networks are rewiring old-school methods such as outbound sales, inbound marketing, sales intelligence, and targeted advertising.

You'll tap into never-before-shared data about how ELG networks have skyrocketed to global scale in the past five years, multiplying from nothing to tens of thousands of companies strong.

You'll learn how to overcome the objections of those who resist change and how to inspire confidence in the security and trust vectors that underlie any successful ELG strategy.

You'll see groundbreaking outcomes in sales efficiency, scalability, demand generation, churn reduction, and product-market fit, all told by the companies that experienced them.

I hope this book provides a glimpse into the excitement and passion that my team and I feel every single day as we work with tech leaders to bring ELG to life in their companies.

I'm thrilled to take you on this journey, and the best time to start is right now. So let's begin.

PART 1

My $2.6 Billion Mistake

1 Muscle Memory and Scar Tissue

When people ask me why repeat start-up founders are more likely to succeed, I say it's because they've developed a healthy mix of muscle memory and scar tissue—and they're willing to admit which is which.

The muscle memory comes from discipline, routines, and skills that are finely tuned over tens of thousands of hours of execution. The scar tissue comes from being wrong. A lot. It builds up during the countless times when, despite all that hard work, everything still goes sideways.

I happen to have a scar bigger than the GDP of Belize.

In June of 2019, a headline flashed across my phone, and I knew one of my most serious business missteps had finally been realized: Google had purchased Looker for $2.6 billion.

Back when Looker was founded in 2012, I was already four years into building a business intelligence software company called RJMetrics. Looker quickly became our main competitor in the space. They had a great product, and their team was first-class. Even so, I was disappointed at the outcome: we had all of those things *plus* a four-year head start.

We ultimately sold RJMetrics to Magento in a modest transaction that was orders of magnitude away from the $2.6 billion windfall earned by Looker. What was the difference between our companies?

It's easy to blame the "muscle memory" stuff—they had more experienced founders and marquee investors, and they just executed better. All true, but were those factors so much better than ours that it led to a 100x difference in outcome? No, there was something much bigger and more profound at play.

Understanding what happened, and the fundamental difference between RJMetrics and Looker, would take me on a fascinating journey of discovery and realization—one that led me to first encounter the ecosystem-led growth playbook and then laid the groundwork for Crossbeam itself.

A Revolution in Business Intelligence

This gets nerdy, but I promise the payoff is worth it. My journey in the world of business intelligence software is how the ecosystem-led growth playbook came to be.

Let's start at the beginning. If you rewind the clock just a decade or so, the analytics needs of a modern business operator were undergoing some major changes.

Take Dave Eisenberg, who in 2010 was chief of staff at an upstart e-commerce menswear shop called Bonobos. Like any smart leader, he wanted to understand his customer lifetime value (CLV) and calculate the return on investment (ROI) of his acquisition channels. To do this kind of analysis, he needed to use several sources of data:

- Data from his ad networks to know how much Bonobos spent per click on different campaigns;
- Data from his marketing platforms to know which emails were sent to which people at what times;
- Data from his web analytics to tell him which visitors were referred from which sources;
- Data from his shopping cart to tell him who bought what, when they did it, and how much they paid; and
- Data from his payment provider to make sure he stripped out any discounts, refunds, or chargebacks.

None of these data sources could run the analysis Dave wanted on its own, because they were all "silos" that couldn't see into the other sources. Getting the answer meant that Dave needed to join all the data together in a separate, central location.

What Dave needed was called **business intelligence (BI) software**, a massive category that had existed for decades. Traditional BI software—which was the only real option for most of its history—consisted of three important components, often bundled up and sold together by a single vendor:

1. Software to **extract, transform, and load (ETL)** data out of all those pesky platforms and into a new, central storage location;
2. A **data warehouse**—the storage location in question—able to handle tons of data ("big data" in early 2000s parlance) and answer analytical queries quickly; and
3. A **reporting interface** where you could build charts and dashboards that display the resulting data and are accessed by your business users.

Any viable business intelligence offering consisted of all three of these pieces in some form or another (see Figure 1.1). Together, they were a singular stack of technology and data, all in one place from one vendor, that allowed a company to be run in a data-driven way.

Because of the scale of data involved, most enterprise deployments had this software deployed "on premise"—physically installed at the location of

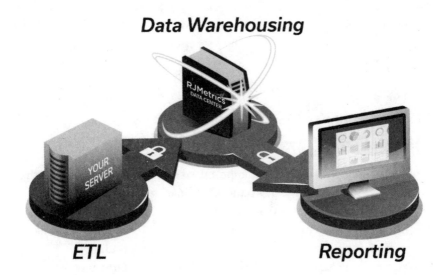

FIGURE 1.1 Artwork from RJMetrics website, ca. 2011.

the business and its end users. Players such as Microstrategy, Cognos, and Business Objects ruled the day.

But Dave was trying to build a modern, web-first company. Plopping an expensive server on premise and running desktop software to crunch his data felt like an anachronism. This was especially true in a moment when the shockwaves of the Great Financial Crisis were still affecting the start-up funding environment and upstarts such as Bonobos needed to squeeze as much **capital efficiency** out of their operations as possible.

It was use cases like Dave's that gave us the idea for RJMetrics. My cofounder Jake Stein and I dreamed of taking the classic on-premise BI paradigms and reinventing them in the cloud.

Your ETL scripts? We'll run them on our servers and have them extract your data from the most widely used online tools to allow for analysis on our platform.

Your data warehouse? We can spin up a free open source database called *MySQL*, host it for you on a server that we manage, and optimize it to run fast analytical queries.

Your reporting layer? Forget finicky desktop software that has to be installed on every client machine. You'll be able to log in from any web browser and create, manage, and distribute the charts and dashboards that make your business tick.

Jake and I quit our jobs in 2008, and RJMetrics was born. Dave at Bonobos became one of our first 10 customers, and hundreds more would soon follow.

The Rollercoaster of Product-Market Fit

Product-market fit (PMF) is the promised land for start-ups. It's that moment at which you have a product that lines up so perfectly with what the market wants and needs that the demand becomes **organic** and undeniable, yielding you the makings of unstoppable growth. PMF can't be faked, and no meaningful company can be built without first finding it.

In our early days at RJMetrics, we were inspired by start-up blogger Eric Reis, who preached the virtues of an efficient "build, measure, learn" cycle for navigating to success. (Reis would later coin the term *The Lean Startup* and author a legendary book of the same name.)

Our lean start-up journey took nearly two years of diligent work and iteration, but it paid off. By 2010, we found our product-market fit (see Figure 1.2).

The deals and the dollars came pouring in faster than we could process them. Our software was flying off the shelves, used by virtually every high-growth e-commerce company in the world. From Bonobos to Fab.com to Rent the Runway and hundreds of others, RJMetrics was ubiquitous among the jet set of next-generation commerce.

Until it wasn't.

We learned a key lesson about product-market fit the hard way. Achieving PMF is not just about iterating on your product; it's also about keeping your product in sync with the market. If the market moves, but your product doesn't move with it, you can lose your fit, and your growth will stop.

At RJMetrics, we got so blinded by the demand for our product that we didn't see a more meaningful evolution in our space happening right underneath our feet. In a span of just a few years, we went from ahead of

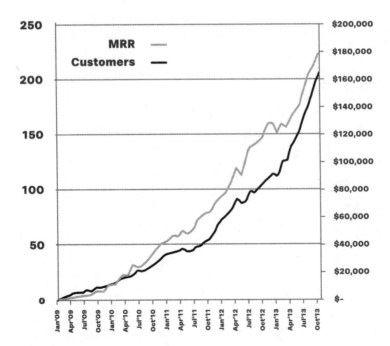

FIGURE 1.2 RJMetrics revenue and customer growth: the bootstrap years.

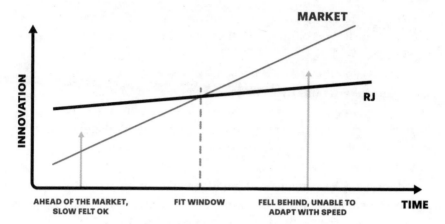

FIGURE 1.3 In product-market fit, the market moves too.

the times to strong PMF to behind the times (see Figure 1.3). By the time we were ready to admit it, we had already lost.

So what happened? What could possibly change a market so radically that an emerging leader could lose its mojo in such a short period of time?

The era of the ecosystem came to our space. And we didn't get on board.

2

Disruption Is Cool Until It Happens to You

Amazon's Big Move

At RJMetrics, by the time we realized we were losing, we had already lost. The same pace of market innovation that made our product a hit had continued under our feet so rapidly that it made us a dinosaur just as fast.

The first domino to fall came from Amazon Web Services (AWS). In late 2012, they announced a new product called Redshift (see Figure 2.1). It was a "fast and powerful, fully managed, petabyte-scale data warehouse service in the cloud."

Remember that cool custom build of MySQL that we developed at RJMetrics? The one that sat right at the center of our technology offering and served as the central location where data was stored, processed, and analyzed? As it turned out, our data warehouse was the horse-and-buggy version of Redshift's Model T.

A study published by SiSense around that time (see Figure 2.2) summed it up plainly: "On average, Redshift was 500x faster than [traditional databases] for metrics like Daily Revenue, Daily Active Users, and Daily ARPU [average revenue per user]."

Yikes. These kinds of "metric queries"—ones about revenue, user activity, and average revenue per user (ARPU)—were precisely the kinds of metrics you could find in RJMetrics. Now you could get them 500x faster if you stored your data in Redshift instead.

FIGURE 2.1 Amazon Redshift announcement release, November 2012.

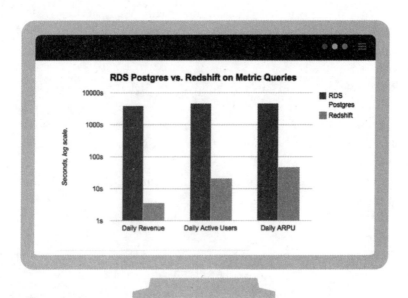

FIGURE 2.2 SiSense benchmarking study outputs, 2015.
Note: "RDS Postgres" is a cloud-deployed competitor to MySQL that was comparable to the RJMetrics data warehouse at the time.

We convinced ourselves that this new technology, while remarkable, wouldn't affect us. Why? Because the data warehouse was just one piece of the puzzle. BI software like ours had a lot more to it. Amazon didn't offer any data pipeline software to extract, transform, and load (ETL) data into its warehouse, nor did they offer a reporting layer for building out your analytics and presenting them to users. Those were big gaps to fill. Weren't they?

Well, as it turned out, a 500x performance improvement, combined with the ease of setup that came with AWS cloud deployments, proved to be enough to drive a major paradigm shift in how companies did analytics. In under three years, Redshift went from a new product to "the fastest growing service in the history of AWS" (see Figure 2.3).

Redshift proved most popular among engineers, data scientists, IT leaders, and professionals in the emerging field of "data ops," all of whom saw tremendous value in keeping control over their company's data. By having a centralized data warehouse located in your AWS cloud and managed by your own ops team, you could exercise unprecedented control over data usage, consistency, cost, and more. It was an exciting proposition for enterprises on countless dimensions.

Cut back to RJMetrics. Here's what we started hearing on sales and renewal calls:

- "Yeah, this looks great, but our data team is telling us that we already have all this data in a data warehouse over at AWS. Why should we also pipe all that same data outside of our cloud over into yours so you can analyze it?"
- "We set up RJMetrics, but the results are just a little different from what our IT people see when they query our Redshift warehouse. Can you do an audit to get those reconciled?"
- "Can we just use your charts and dashboards on top of our warehouse instead?"

I recently caught up with Vijay Subramanian, who was chief analytics officer and head of growth at Rent the Runway. They were a marquee customer of ours at RJMetrics who churned off of our platform in this pivotal era.

"RJMetrics was used to report on our key user and growth metrics, but as we started tracking other parts of the business, we felt the need to pipe it

FIGURE 2.3 *The Register* headline, April 2015.

FIGURE 2.4 When we lost the warehouse, we lost our way.

all into a common warehouse where we could manage more of the nuanced business modeling," he reminisced. "RJMetrics struggled to serve our needs as it was an all-in-one solution."

Our data warehouse was a loser (see Figure 2.4). And when we lost the warehouse wars, it literally snapped our value proposition right down the middle. The other two ends of our product just couldn't hold up the product-market fit chasm in the middle.

The Modern Data Stack Is Born

Former Netscape CEO Jim Barksdale famously said that there are "only two ways to make money in business: one is to bundle; the other is to unbundle." Between 2013 and 2016, we experienced a radical unbundling in the way data was moved, processed, analyzed, and consumed by modern businesses. In the process, it forged one of the most powerful and valuable partner ecosystems ever to exist, exposing me to the ecosystem-led growth playbooks that would change my career forever.

Within a year of Redshift's release, the traditional business intelligence approach of an all-in-one analytics stack had been split apart. In its wake, a new generation of companies emerged that took on the rest of the stack piecemeal.

Depending on how you count it, somewhere between five and ten new categories of software and services seemed to emerge overnight. These companies each took over a slice of the old all-in-one stack and, when combined, gave end users a "modern data stack" that could be seamlessly integrated to provide more power, flexibility, and affordability than anything that came before.

Data warehouse innovation didn't stop with Redshift. Google and Microsoft soon answered with BigQuery and Azure Data Warehouse, respectively. Later, Snowflake's powerful data warehousing offering won it a dominant position as one of the fastest growing and highest valued SaaS companies ever with a peak market value of $118 billion.

ETL platforms such as Fivetran and Matillion arrived, whose main purpose was to move data between leading SaaS platforms and the warehouses listed above. In a 2021 funding round, Fivetran was valued at $5.6 billion.

Reporting platforms narrowed their scope to focus on nailing the data modeling and dashboarding capabilities. This is where Looker focused. In the modern data stack era, a wave of new vendors came to market in this space including Looker, Mode, Periscope, Redash, Hex, and Omni. Legacy application players such as Tableau also entered the space with more robust cloud offerings. In 2019, Tableau was acquired by Salesforce for $15.7 billion and Looker was acquired by Google for $2.6 billion.

Other layers surrounding these tools—such as transformation workflow solutions including dbt ("data build tool")—have also emerged and come to meaningful scale. In a 2022 round of funding, dbt Labs was valued at $4.2 billion.

In addition to software innovation, an entire industry of services businesses, **agency partners**, and system integrators emerged around this market as well (see Figure 2.5). Especially with enterprise deployments, the value of human experts to pull these pieces together, train teams, and deploy best practices are more important than ever.

Just incredible. So many new markets that they're hard to count, each with new incumbents that didn't exist a decade ago—all valued at billions.

And with that, a new industry emerged with a bang, and RJMetrics would be sold off with a whimper.

The Ecosystem Effect

It's now clear as day how Looker grew to 100x our value in half of the time: they grew as part of an emerging and highly disruptive ecosystem while we flew solo.

"The partner ecosystem was one of our superpowers," Keenan Rice shared with me in a recent conversation. Rice was a member of Looker's founding team and served as a vice president of Sales, Marketing, and eventually Global Partnerships at the company. "We found our place developing and coleading a powerful ecosystem at a critical time in the larger data sector, and those partner relationships catapulted us to the top of our category."

Looker didn't just make its partners' products more valuable—its use was predicated on their use. It made co-selling and using partner products an existential requirement for its customers. In turn, the same was true in the opposite direction. They built together, they sold together, and they won together.

Meanwhile, any company still trying to go solo fizzled out. At RJMetrics, what felt like a strategic advantage—we were a one-stop shop, the only thing you would need—ended up being our downfall.

The tale of the modern data stack and its disruptive effects on incumbents such as RJMetrics is not a one-off. In fact, it was just a canary in the coal mine of the entire software industry.

Data has become more structured, portable, and well-suited to product integrations, and in turn the DNA of the software value proposition has been rearranged. Who you partner with, and how, has gone from a curiosity

The Modern Data Stack

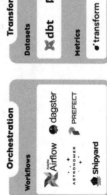
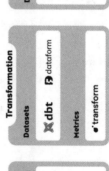

FIGURE 2.5 The modern data stack map by Valentin Umbach.
Source: Adapted from @ValentinUmbach on X.

19

question to a core tenet of how purchasing decisions get made and value gets delivered.

The services industry has likewise adapted to this trend, with even the largest global system integrators now consulting on the best ways to buy, integrate, and deploy stacks of synergistic software as opposed to monolithic deployments of a single tool. In a world where your value story is inextricably tied to your partner ecosystem, so too is your growth strategy and the tools at your disposal to pursue it.

This leads us to a powerful conclusion: partner ecosystems will be the most prolific and efficient growth lever businesses can build in the modern era. We're already seeing the winners of this era start to emerge. Every thriving venture scale company in the modern era is doing these two things well:

1. Building compelling software that delivers its specific value proposition to a specific user persona; and
2. Seamlessly integrating their value proposition with the complementary products and services that exist in their market.

Countless think pieces have been written about doing that first bullet well. This book is about the second one: ecosystem-led growth.

In today's technology landscape, your place in an ecosystem of partners is just as important, if not more so, than the quality of your product itself. Marc Andreessen was right when he proclaimed that "software is eating the world." But in today's marketplace, ecosystems are eating software.

3 How Partner Ecosystems Saved My Career

RJMetrics was sold to Magento in 2016 in a modest transaction. In the deal negotiation, however, we did architect a silver lining.

Magento was most interested in owning the reporting layer of our product, and we were able to negotiate the ability to keep our data pipeline technology, which we had started selling on its own as "RJMetrics Pipeline." We spun that technology out into a new company, Stitch Data (see Figure 3.1).

Stitch was one of the first players in the ETL layer of the modern data stack. That's right, Jake and I became a part of the very ecosystem that had just wiped us off the map. Even more ironically, we soon formed huge partnerships with the likes of Looker and AWS, the exact products that had precipitated our demise.

Stitch was all ecosystem, no silos. We were basically data-plumbing "middleware," and most of the end users who benefited from Stitch didn't even know it existed. We pulled in data from the SaaS tools and databases you used and deposited it into a data warehouse of your choice, quickly and accurately.

In a massive ecosystem with SaaS tools on one side and data warehousing platforms on the other, Stitch made everyone else's products better. And all those partners sent hordes of customers our way.

Our growth strategy incorporated the following:

- We co-marketed with our SaaS partners whose ideal customer profile overlapped perfectly with ours and whose products became more

FIGURE 3.1 Stitch launch blog post, August 2016.

valuable and harder to stop using when our shared customers used Stitch to connect their data to analytics tools.

- We co-sold with our data warehouse and analytics partners whose customers got more value and opened up more use cases when we moved new sources of data into their products.
- We grew revenue based on data volume, and our partners grew revenue based on consumption and use cases. We helped each other reduce churn and drive best-in-class expansion numbers.

In just 28 months, Stitch grew as big as RJMetrics did over eight years—and we did it with a quarter of the headcount and no new outside funding. Every single dollar of revenue was tied inextricably to our graph of partners and the value proposition we provided together.

We were acquired by Talend in November 2018 for $60 million in cash, and my love affair with partner ecosystems was cast in stone.

By 2018 I was convinced that an ecosystem-driven transformation was coming for every company in tech. It hurt us at RJMetrics and was rocket fuel at Stitch. It was well on its way to revolutionizing how companies build products, and the inevitable next wave would see it transform how those businesses drive efficient, scalable growth.

The RJMetrics and Stitch story wasn't a one-off. Everywhere I looked, the same patterns were taking hold:

- Buyers of technology were prioritizing strong partner ecosystems and technical extensibility as table-stakes part of any product's feature set.
- The highest-potential new companies were part of interconnected "stacks" of compatible technologies that delivered better value together.
- Go-to-market motions were evolving in a way that put partner relationships and value stories front and center.
- The largest technology companies in the world were aggressively investing in partner ecosystem fundamentals such as **application programming interfaces (APIs)** that could be used to build connectivity to other products, co-selling initiatives, and marketplaces.

The massive disruption caused by the modern API economy and the late stages of the digital transformation movement were pushing cloud and SaaS adoption even into the slowest-moving enterprises. Then, ecosystem dynamics were affecting value stories and purchasing behavior more significantly than ever.

From marketing technology ("martech") to e-commerce to cloud computing and even traditional industries outside of tech, it was the same story. This ecosystem effect was unstoppable and on its way to ubiquity.

Harnessing the power of these tectonic shifts would require a new kind of growth strategy. Done right, it could transform a company's partner ecosystem into its most prolific, scalable, and efficient source of customers and revenue.

This strategy would come to be known as ecosystem-led growth (ELG), a new go-to-market motion that focuses on partner ecosystems as the primary way to attract, convert, and grow customer relationships.

There was just one problem: the practitioners of this craft needed help. There were massive holes in the data layer needed to make ELG work at scale, existing partnership software was a relic from a bygone era, and the best practices of the industry were poorly documented (if at all).

Thus began the journey to unpack, understand, and help rewrite the dynamics of partnerships, ecosystems, and the strategies that have shaped them over the course of modern tech history.

Up next, we'll retrace these steps, looking at where we've been, the technology that has emerged as a result, and the historic moments when ELG came into its own.

PART 2

The Ecosystem Revolution

4

Decoding the Confusing Language of Partnerships

"MSP? ISV? PRM? WTF? IDK."

—Every new partnerships person ever

Having now explored the advances in software and data technology that make ecosystem-led growth possible, we're left with just one more piece of the puzzle to understand: the history of partnerships themselves. In this chapter, we'll demystify the language and history of partnerships, positioning ecosystem-led growth as a major evolutionary step in how and why companies partner.

The partnerships function has existed for a long time, and along the way it has accumulated more than its share of overloaded terms, three-letter acronyms, and dense jargon. Some new partnership professionals spend weeks or months internalizing it all, but this chapter is a crash course designed to make you fluent in just a few minutes. We'll explore the labels applied to different partnership types and the technology traditionally used by partner teams.

Many of the concepts in this chapter predate the modern software economy and the ecosystem-led growth movement. For that reason, we refer to these concepts as legacy terms and technologies.

I must confess that I find the state of jargon, acronyms, and vocabulary in the legacy partnerships space to be a frustrating mess. If you spend your career in one particular ecosystem or sector, you may end up very opinionated about what each one of these terms means and how it is defined—only

27

to meet someone at a conference with a totally different worldview and get lost in your conflicting vocabularies. But it's all made up.

There are tens of thousands of working professionals who trade in this dense jargon as if it were a second language. Giving these folks the benefit of the doubt, it's just the language of their trade that has racked up linguistic debt over decades of evolution. Taking a more cynical eye, however, it is also a form of gatekeeping.

The jargon density of the traditional partnerships space makes it incredibly hard for outside stakeholders to follow along, young talent to navigate conversations, and new movements to disrupt the status quo. It can feel like a form of "job security by obscurity" for an enormous and lucrative piece of the world economy.

That's why you should get smart on what all this stuff means, even if you plan to throw it all out the window. In this chapter, we'll build up the table stakes language you need to classify different partnership types and motions so you and your team can tuck it in neatly into your own company's strategy, answer questions from the outside about how it all fits together, and ultimately recast the discussion under the one term that covers them all: ecosystem-led growth (ELG).

Let's start simply: a **partner** is an outside company, organization, or person with whom you "win together." Typically, these wins are achieved because you have shared customers, markets, and/or goals. Partners have some direct economic incentive to help you win, which can be quite diverse in nature. Generating new business, increasing the loyalty of existing customers, earning commissions, and building relationship capital are all common incentives at play.

This is different from your **vendors** (that is, accountants, lawyers, SaaS tools you buy), who are paid directly by you to provide a service back to you. It's also not the same as your **customers**, who are transacting directly with you to buy your product. Partners are a distinct beast. They are more like a third party in a "value triangle" with a shared customer, user, or **stakeholder**.

A **partner ecosystem** is an interconnected network of businesses, communities, and individuals that work together and often rely on each other to offer end-to-end value to their shared customers or prospects.

The partners in your ecosystem could integrate technology, offer services or solutions that enhance your offering, or simply resell or distribute your products. No matter what they do for you—and we'll dissect the different types in a moment—this universe of companies has a simple thing in common: they win when you win.

In the modern business world, partner ecosystems have become so prolific, interconnected, and important that they are often referred to simply as *ecosystems* for short.

Thus, **ecosystem-led growth** is a go-to-market motion that focuses on the partner ecosystem as the primary way to attract, convert, and grow customer relationships.

As a differentiated go-to-market motion, ELG leverages your network of partners, communities, and marketplaces. It does this via data, technology, and processes to drive growth at scale, in essence operationalizing the value of the data and relationships in your ecosystem.

Unlike direct sales or marketing, ELG is infinitely scalable. It allows you to expand your market reach by orders of magnitude rather than linearly. ELG also delivers on operationalizing these indirect channels at scale by using data, automation, and brand-new playbooks.

Initially, you may think of your company's ecosystem as a big hub-and-spoke diagram, with your company at the center of many partnerships that revolve around (see Figure 4.1).

As it turns out, however, virtually no one's ecosystem is shaped like this—and that's a good thing. In reality, a healthy ecosystem contains many companies that each have *their own ecosystem* as well.

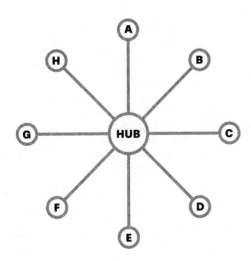

FIGURE 4.1 Hub and spoke.

In other words, while you may consider yourself the hub in your ecosystem, you have to remember that you are also a spoke in each of your partners' ecosystems. Even more important is that many of your partners may in fact also be partnered with *each other* in addition to their partnerships with you.

As a result, ecosystems aren't hubs and spokes at all. They're network graphs (see Figure 4.2).

This network graph ecosystem shape is far more robust than the hub and spoke, and the density of connections inside of that graph are a desirable healthy characteristic of any ecosystem. "Density" in this case is simply the number of connections within the graph itself. Higher density means that the average company in your ecosystem also itself has a healthy ecosystem and that a large number of its partners are also your partners.

Remember the modern data stack from my RJMetrics story? That's the definition of a dense ecosystem. Countless SaaS companies are partnered with every ETL tool to extract data. Every ETL tool then partners with every data warehouse to store the data. Then every data warehouse partners with every business intelligence tool to display the data. And so on.

In the modern data stack, the density is off the charts. You can see this in just a tiny subset of the network graph for Snowflake, a leading data warehouse (see Figure 4.3).

Snowflake is a monster company, but their ecosystem is no hub and spoke. It's extremely dense and reflects the maturity, stability, and promise of the industry in which it exists.

The density of connections in this ecosystem means that Snowflake is likely no farther than one existing connection away from any new partner

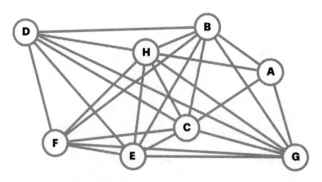

FIGURE 4.2 Network graph.

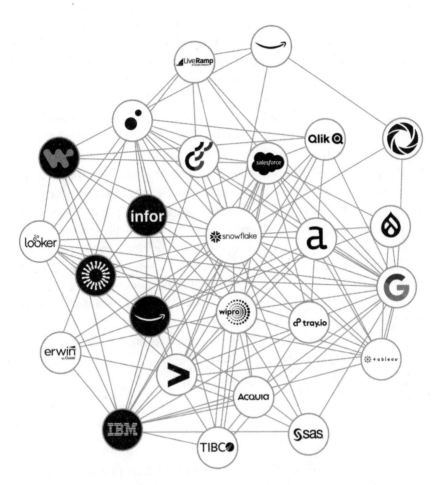

FIGURE 4.3 Snowflake's high-density partner ecosystem via partnerbase.com.

it might want to pursue. It also has plenty of redundancy, meaning that even if companies disappear, get acquired, or change their models, there are plenty of others in the "mesh" with similar connective tissue that can grow to fill the void left behind.

In this way, partner networks are a resilient and self-healing fabric that grows exponentially with a company's industry, target markets, and use cases. In your ecosystem, you're the "Kevin Bacon" that's never more than six degrees away from the perfect contact or information to move your business forward.

The website partnerbase.com, a free online directory created by Crossbeam, tracks these partner ecosystems and the rich interconnectedness between them. If you want to get your fill of dense network graphs, including one for your own company, it's a great free resource.

But here's where the jargon starts to creep in. The definition of *partner* mentioned earlier is so broad that it allows for a huge universe of partner types to exist, each with their own specific flavor of value creation.

Maybe you've heard someone use the phrase *channel partners* interchangeably with *go-to-market partners* or heard someone slip *ISV* into a conversation about their tech integrations. Or perhaps your eyes have glazed over as an industry vet rattled off stories of dealing with MSPs, SIs, and VARs. Or maybe you spilled your Scrabble tiles on the ground once.

What follows is a breakdown of the most common partnership types and the alphabet soup of these acronyms that you may hear as you dip your toes into building your own ecosystem. We'll try to use all these sparingly in this book, but it's worth familiarizing yourself if you want to achieve ecosystem mastery.

We'll classify the universe of partnerships into three mega-buckets and drill in from there. Those are tech partnerships, channel partnerships, and strategic partnerships.

Tech Partnerships

Broadly speaking, if a partnership involves your tech product integrating with your partner's tech product, you have a **technology** (or simply **tech**) **partnership** on your hands. This is also referred to as an *integration partnership*, or simply a *tech integration*.

Most tech partnerships, especially in software, can also be referred to as **independent software vendor** (**ISV**) partnerships. This moniker applies in cases where the two companies are distinct entities that each have their own customer relationships, and they bring elevated value to their joint customers via their tech integrations.

While companies in the technology industry develop software to solve a specific problem, they simply can't address every need for their customers. If they do, they may sacrifice quality in their search to become an all-in-one solution, and they may lose customers who prefer best-in-breed tools in their tech stack. This is where tech partners come in.

Generally, the more value journeys a platform supports, the more valuable it becomes to the end user or customer. ISVs integrate some of the functionality or features of their own software within their partner's platform, thus making the platform a more well-rounded, comprehensive solution.

Tech partnerships can be critical to a company's growth because they enable both partners to enter new, adjacent markets without investing heavily in new product developments.

When a company such as Spotify develops an application that runs on Amazon Alexa devices, they are embarking on a tech partnership. The ability to use a simple voice command to listen to Spotify on any Amazon Alexa device increases the value of both Spotify and Alexa, to the mutual benefit of their shared customers.

With this tech partnership in place, shared customers of Alexa and Spotify become more loyal to both products. Once the integration is activated by the end user, the products have made each other more deeply entrenched in the end user's experience. Among other things, this makes them each more painful to remove—a trait that some product managers call "stickiness." Moving away from Alexa would cut down on the devices and locations in which Spotify can be streamed. Moving away from Spotify would diminish the value of having an Alexa device in every room. The partnership seeds a symbiotic relationship between these products—they are a part of each other's value stories.

Another dead-simple (and very fun) example of a tech partnership is the Giphy Slack app.

Giphy is a search engine for GIFs, mostly of the meme variety. Among other things, it's my personal go-to when I really need that GIF of Homer Simpson ghosting backward into the bushes. Giphy is wildly popular, and its growth has been accelerated by the universe of tech partnerships it has forged. These integrations, now embedded in everything from Facebook to Adobe to Slack, put Giphy's GIFs at the fingertips of just about every Internet consumer on the planet.

The Slack app is a tech partnership that provides Giphy with distribution to millions of business users and enhances the experience of using Slack by adding a fun, fast, and rich library of GIFs to the vocabulary of its users.

The lucrative world of **business-to-business software as a service (B2B SaaS)** is rich with tech partnerships. Take DocuSign, the largest platform for electronic signatures and agreements.

DocuSign is an ISV partner of Salesforce, with which they developed an integration to enable companies of all sizes and across industries to "go paperless" and sync their document management processes with their Salesforce **customer relationship management (CRM)** data.

Salesforce customers can benefit from unifying their contracts and other documentation with their CRM data—thus, making Salesforce a more complete solution for their business needs. Meanwhile, DocuSign benefits by gaining access to Salesforce's 150,000+ customer base from directly inside the Salesforce user interface (see Figure 4.4).

A great place to find more examples of tech partnerships is on a company's partner page, sometimes called the **app store** or the **integration** marketplace of large tech platforms. The Salesforce AppExchange, Shopify App Store, and Zapier Integration List are treasure troves of tech partnerships.

It should be noted that there are some tech partnerships that fall outside of the ISV designation. Most notable are **original equipment manufacturer (OEM)** partnerships.

FIGURE 4.4 DocuSign in Salesforce.

This acronym is funny to me—it reminds me of the fact that we still use a picture of the floppy disk as the "save" icon even though no one born in the past 25 years even knows what a floppy disk is. So too does the term *original equipment manufacturer* somehow persist to describe a partnership motion that often doesn't involve equipment or manufacturers at all.

OEM partnerships come into play when one product creator fully and often opaquely embeds another company's product within its own. That other company is the "original manufacturer" of the "equipment" being embedded.

A traditional example might be the use of Intel chips in Dell PCs or the use of Corning's Gorilla Glass as the screen material in iPhones. Intel and Corning are effectively making a sale every time Dell or Apple makes a sale—they just don't share the branding glory.

Within modern tech ecosystems, OEM-style partnerships are often synonymous with **white labeling**, in which one company's software is embedded in another's without the end user needing to know or realize that they are using a partner company's technology. Contrast this to most ISV partnerships where the end user must be a customer of both companies to use the integration.

A powerful example of an OEM motion in modern SaaS is embedded analytics. Nearly every modern SaaS platform has a need for charts, reporting, and other metrics within their product. Whether it's there to show usage data or statistics about the impacts of the software being used, the prevalence of a "reporting" tab is quite high.

Enter Sigma Computing, a leader in the modern business intelligence space. SaaS companies that use Sigma's Embedded Analytics product can offer world-class reporting within their own products without having to build all the complex machinery on their own from the ground up. According to their website, this helps "increase your product's stickiness and value-add by providing your customers with easy self-serve access to their data within your product."

In true OEM fashion, a Sigma-powered reporting feature looks and feels like a part of the partner's product, but behind the scenes Sigma is powering a special embedded dashboard for each customer that contains only their data.

It's noteworthy that OEM relationships are definitionally commercial to some degree. Dell is buying those Intel chips, Apple is buying that Corning Gorilla Glass, and Sigma is charging for those embedded dashboards.

But there is a texture to this kind of relationship that earns it a place at the partnerships table—these companies win together.

Channel Partnerships

Your **channel partners** include any and all outside companies that assist you in marketing, selling, or delivering your products or services to your customers. They are quite literally a "channel" through which your product gets sold or delivered.

This is distinct from a tech partnership in that most channel partners do not have a technology product themselves but instead exist in the service industry and make money by helping their customers procure, implement, and maintain the product offerings of other companies.

Because of this, channel partner relationships are often more directional in nature, consisting of the **vendor** (a software company or business that manufactures the product being purchased) and the **partner** (the business that is selling or servicing the product).

Contrast this to ISV partnerships, in which both parties are a "vendor" and the nature of the partnership is that they are enhancing each other's products as opposed to taking on responsibility for selling or servicing them.

In most cases, a channel relationship involves a **co-branding relationship** between you and that partner, in which you each preserve brand awareness and the customer is still aware they are consuming your product despite it being sold or serviced by a third party.

There are numerous subcategories of channel partners, and while their definitions are distinct, the lines between them can get extremely blurry and some channel partners can fit into multiple labels.

Take resellers. In the context of channel partnerships, a **reseller partner** is a company or individual that purchases a product or service from the original manufacturer or service provider and then sells it to their customers, often with added value or services. Resellers play a crucial role in the distribution and sales process, helping manufacturers extend their reach and tap into new markets. By leveraging their existing networks, industry expertise, and sales capabilities, resellers can effectively promote and sell products to a broader audience.

One notable example of a software reseller is CDW, a Fortune 500 company that offers **information technology** (**IT**) solutions to businesses, governments, and educational institutions. CDW partners with leading technology companies such as Microsoft, Adobe, and Cisco to resell their software and hardware products. In 2020, CDW reported net sales of over $18 billion, showcasing the significant impact resellers can have on the software industry.

Another prominent software reseller is Insight Enterprises, a global provider of IT solutions and services. Insight partners with major software vendors such as Microsoft, VMware, and IBM, offering customers access to a wide range of software products and services. In 2020, Insight Enterprises reported annual revenue of over $8.3 billion.

Now, what happens when a reseller does more than just resell a product that was built by another company? They morph into something greater— and we go deeper into the jargon.

Value-added resellers (VARs), distributors, managed service providers (MSPs), and system integrators (SIs) are all types of channel partners in the software industry, but they differ in their focus and the services they provide.

Value-added resellers (VARs) are companies that purchase software or hardware products from manufacturers and then sell them to their customers, often bundled with additional services such as installation, configuration, and customization. VARs add value to the original product by tailoring it to the specific needs of their customers, which differentiates them from traditional resellers. A notable example of a VAR is SHI International, a global IT solutions provider that partners with major technology vendors such as Microsoft, Adobe, and Dell. In 2021, SHI International reported annual revenue of over $12.3 billion.

Distributors are a special kind of reseller that typically do not sell directly to end users. Instead, they sit in the middle between manufacturers and other resellers or retailers who interface with the end consumer of the product. Ingram Micro is a well-known distributor whose business model is largely based on acting as an intermediary between manufacturers and resellers of technology products. In doing so, Ingram Micro helps manufacturers reach a broader audience while providing resellers with a wide range of products and logistical support. (Confusingly, Ingram Micro and many of its distributor ilk also offer value-added services and are sometimes labeled as a VAR. In case you haven't noticed yet, these channel partnership distinctions get quite blurry and are rarely mutually exclusive.)

Managed service providers (MSPs) are companies or organizations that specialize in overseeing and managing specific operational processes or functions on behalf of other businesses. In tech, they are commonly associated with IT services, such as network management, security, and technical support. But MSPs exist in more traditional industries too, from facilities management to accounting outsourcing to health care management.

Still with me? Most of the channel partnership acronyms are now under our belt—just one to go!

Let's talk **system integrators (SIs)**. These are companies that specialize in integrating diverse IT systems, software applications, and hardware components into a cohesive and functional whole. SIs help organizations streamline their IT infrastructure and ensure seamless interoperability between different systems. There are two types of SIs: **global system integrators (GSIs)** and **regional system integrators (RSIs)**.

Global system integrators (GSIs) are large, multinational companies that operate across multiple industries and geographies. Examples of GSIs include Accenture, Deloitte, and IBM Global Services—and they're all behemoths. In 2020, Accenture alone reported annual revenue of over $44 billion.

Regional system integrators (RSIs), on the other hand, are smaller companies that operate within specific geographic areas or industries. These SIs offer tailored solutions and services to local customers, leveraging their regional expertise and knowledge.

Whether or not a given company fits the profile of an SI, GSI, or RSI is often debatable. Sometimes their partners do the work of classifying them, sometimes they classify themselves, and sometimes they have their hands in so many different cookie jars that they defy consistent classification at all.

Strategic Partnerships

Strategic partnerships, also known as **strategic alliances**, are the big eye-catchers in partnerships. They can encompass any of the partnership types mentioned earlier but do so with long-term, big-picture planning and intention.

Strategic partnerships often involve a higher level of commitment and trust, as both parties work together to achieve common goals, enhance their market positions, or tackle new business opportunities. Buyer beware, however—a "strategic" partnership can also be a clever way to grab headlines or send a message to the market long before actually doing any of the work that makes it valuable.

Here are a few examples that illustrate the distinct nature of strategic partnerships and some recent examples of note.

Joint product development: Strategic partners often collaborate on developing new products or enhancing existing ones, creating unique offerings that can differentiate them in the market. In 2017, Adobe and Microsoft announced a strategic partnership to integrate Adobe's marketing cloud with Microsoft's Dynamics 365 CRM platform. This collaboration allowed both companies to deliver a comprehensive marketing and sales solution, enabling their customers to better manage customer relationships and drive business growth.

Co-marketing initiatives: Strategic partnerships can involve joint marketing efforts to reach a broader audience or target specific market segments. In 2018, Salesforce and Apple announced a strategic partnership to bring together the power of Salesforce's CRM platform with iOS, Apple's mobile operating system. This collaboration resulted in a series of co-marketing initiatives, including the development of an SDK (software development kit) for iOS, enabling developers to build native Salesforce apps for iPhone and iPad devices. This partnership allowed both companies to expand their reach and strengthen their positions in their respective markets.

Shared resources and expertise: Strategic partners can pool resources and expertise to tackle complex business challenges or address new opportunities. In 2019, Google Cloud and VMware announced a strategic partnership aimed at helping organizations accelerate their digital transformation journeys. As part of this collaboration, VMware's virtualization and cloud infrastructure solutions were integrated with Google Cloud's platform, enabling customers to leverage both companies' expertise in cloud computing and data center management.

Market expansion: Strategic partnerships can help companies enter new markets or expand their presence in existing ones. In 2021, Slack and Atlassian announced a strategic partnership aimed at deepening their integration and expanding their reach in the enterprise collaboration market. As part of this partnership, Atlassian's popular team collaboration tools, such as Jira and Trello, were integrated with Slack's communication platform, allowing users to seamlessly collaborate across both platforms. This partnership enabled both companies to offer a more comprehensive solution for team collaboration and expand their market presence.

Industry alliances: Strategic partnerships can also take the form of industry alliances that involve multiple players all committing to the same strategic direction and vision. An exciting current example of an industry alliance is the MACH Alliance, a not-for-profit industry body that advocates for open and best-of-breed enterprise technology ecosystems. MACH is an acronym representing the shared technical philosophy of its member companies: Microservices-based, API-first, Cloud-native, and Headless. By aligning around a common standard for how to build powerful and interoperable technology products, the companies in the MACH alliance can win together by sharing knowledge and pushing a joint narrative that informed enterprise buyers should only adopt products that adhere to this standard.

In the end, these strategic partnerships support a bigger and more profound part of the involved companies' strategies than your run-of-the-mill tech or channel partnership. That comes with proportional risks but also the potential for massive upside when the stars align and the vision behind the partnership comes to fruition.

Marketplaces

A marketplace is a venue where buyers and sellers come together to exchange goods or services. Your local farmers market is a marketplace, as is eBay or a neighborhood swap meet.

In the context of modern partnerships, we can narrow that definition quite a bit. For our purposes, a **marketplace** is an online platform where vendors can offer their digital products, services, or solutions to end users. Examples include app stores, cloud service marketplaces, or software plug-in repositories.

Marketplaces are a powerful tool in the modern economy, especially in the context of software, because they serve two important functions at once:

- A discovery mechanism where buyers can find products that meet certain criteria around functionality or compatibility; and
- A point of sale where buyers can transact with the marketplace directly in order to purchase those products.

Marketplace partnerships are the ones that exist between the company that hosts the marketplace and their partners (often called *vendors* or *sellers*) who list their products or services on that marketplace. There is a direct and sometimes complex financial relationship between those parties that involves sales commissions and complex legal interdependencies.

One specific category of marketplaces is worth understanding in the context of ecosystem-led growth: hyperscaler cloud marketplaces. A **hyperscaler** is a massive company such as Amazon, Google, or Microsoft that is aggressively investing to dominate the **public cloud** infrastructure market as well as the economy enabled by it. They have all opened cloud marketplaces where other software products can be purchased.

You can think of a cloud marketplace kind of like the AWS App Store only instead of buying Angry Birds on your iPhone for 99 cents, you're entering into a six-figure contract for a network-monitoring SaaS tool.

Hyperscaler marketplaces are hardly a "before times" concept—quite the contrary, they are one of the largest areas of investment in the current partnership economy. By providing a venue in which to sell cloud technology products, these hyperscalers are gaining even more visibility and control over the cloud economy and the way their customers invest budgets. It's a land grab between the biggest names in tech.

I find it extremely noteworthy and mildly amusing how the requirements to list a product on these marketplaces has loosened up over the years:

- In the early days of these marketplaces, you could only list your product if it was tightly integrated with the underlying hyperscaler cloud and directly resulted in an increase in consumption of cloud infrastructure. An example would be a network-monitoring tool that observed a customer's resources running on the hyperscaler's cloud and required some additional computer or storage resources in that cloud in order to run.
- Later, this was loosened to allow listings from any SaaS provider or service that ran on that hyperscaler's cloud. This could be, say, a CRM platform that happened to be a customer of the hyperscaler and hosted their SaaS tool on its cloud. This made the connection to cloud consumption more indirect and harder to quantify, but there was still a sense that the motivation was to drive more cloud consumption.
- Most recently, these marketplaces have opened up the gates. They've started allowing SaaS tools to list even if they are fully hosted on other, competing cloud platforms. That's right: you can buy a product on one hyperscaler's marketplace that directly results in more consumption happening on a competing marketplace.

Why this change? The strategy has shifted from increasing each hyperscaler's cloud consumption revenue (an incremental but direct benefit) to increasing the hyperscaler's market share of the entire cloud economy. It's a bigger play with bigger network effects that could put the winner in a better power position in the long game.

Partner Relationship Management

The final acronym we'll explore in this chapter is perhaps the most complex and nefarious: PRM.

Partner relationship management (PRM) software is a category name used to describe any software product that helps companies manage and collaborate with their partners. PRMs streamline various aspects of partner management including training, documentation distribution, lead registration, and commission management. It's a catch-all for software that does all the "partner stuff" at a company, and as such it has become an overloaded and confusing term for many.

We count numerous PRM software companies as our partners and friends at Crossbeam, so I enter into this section with some trepidation. But I feel a need to be clear: traditional PRM is a deeply challenged legacy category of software. It is cursed by the need to be a catch-all for solving the needs of partnership teams, yet it's sold to groups with negligible budgets and resources. As a result, very little innovation has emerged in PRM over the last 10 years.

Here, too, we see the bundling/unbundling dynamics we've mentioned before. Your typical PRM system is not so much a unified platform as an amalgam of features that check as many boxes as possible for your typical partner team.

Since the budgets and team sizes in partnerships can't sustain an industry of dozens of unbundled solutions, what instead emerges over time is a small universe of bundled offerings that aim to solve every partnership need under one hood.

And when I say bundled, I mean *bundled*. We will occasionally get miscategorized as a PRM at Crossbeam and asked by analyst groups at Gartner, Forrester, and other firms to fill out questionnaires about what features our "PRM" offers. We don't respond, but the length and diversity of what's on that list is jaw dropping.

In the most recent survey we received from a mainstream analyst group, the list of PRM features was 131 items long. I've consolidated just a small subset of the PRM features they ask vendors about below—see how many otherwise distinct categories of SaaS, each of which contain their own billion-dollar companies, you can count in the list:

- Deal registration;
- Partner contract design, signature, and management;
- Partner portals;
- Partner certification and learning path;
- Partner analytics dashboards including easy customization;
- Video conferencing tools for partner coaching, webinars, and conferencing;
- Partner onboarding;
- "To," "Through," and "With" email marketing campaign capabilities;
- Partner financial incentives including market development funds;
- Partner locator including maps and geolocation;
- Partner account management and territory assignment;
- Partner program compliance manager;
- Management and templates for quarterly business reviews;
- Extensive workflow design and automation capabilities;
- Content management system;
- Automated personalization;
- Social marketing for and with partners;
- Lead distribution and assignment from vendors to partners;
- Landing pages and microsites;
- Support for webinar and event marketing, including event calendars;
- Search engine marketing;
- Invoices;
- Forecasting;
- Commission tracking;
- Knowledge management and database for partners; and
- AI-powered chatbots.

I counted no fewer than 10 distinct business cases there for which massive companies have been built. The typical PRM vendor is somehow expected to build DocuSign, Zoom, QuickBooks, Drift, Clari, Marketo, Hootsuite, Zapier, WordPress, and ChatGPT all under one hood. They are somehow expected to check these boxes, on their own, specifically and exclusively to serve the small underfunded partner teams that consume them. How on earth could it be anything other than chaos? This isn't a software category, it's bedlam.

And so we find that vendors who get to scale are the ones who find the right subset of offerings (unbundling) or audience (targeted personas) to accumulate some kind of scale. Unfortunately, in doing so, they even further limit their total addressable market and put a ceiling on their terminal value.

A few of the more prominent, successful PRM vendors focused on the tech sector are listed below along with their funding and achievement history:

- *Impartner*. Considered one of the most accomplished and exciting players in the bunch, Impartner is a privately held, venture-backed company. Its journey to this stature is over 25 years long, however, as the company was founded in 1997—a full two years before Salesforce itself was founded.
- *Allbound*. Founded in 2014, Allbound is one of the younger companies in the bunch. In its nearly 10-year history, its success has been highly concentrated among smaller tech companies at low price points. It was recapitalized in a $43M transaction in 2022 with private equity firm Invictus Capital.
- *ZINFI Technologies*. Founded in 2007, ZINFI has made a name for itself in the channel partnership space. ZoomInfo estimates its revenue at between $30 and $40 million.
- *Zift Solutions*. A well-known and well-funded player in the PRM space, Zift has gone through several rebrandings and mergers over its history since being founded in 2006. (Its PRM offering was once called Relayware.) ZoomInfo estimated its 2022 revenue at roughly $21 million.
- *Salesforce*. The one gorilla in the PRM room is Salesforce, whose "Sales Cloud PRM" product does a good job of checking off the feature functionality on the previous list and is the leading provider among enterprises. It is a behemoth in the PRM space but such a small percentage of Salesforce revenue that its financials don't meet the reporting requirements for it to be publicly disclosed.

There are dozens of smaller and non-tech-focused players in the greater PRM space, and my apologies for any omissions. But I offer the above list for the purpose of pattern recognition. What we see above is a category littered with players who, despite best intentions, seem to hit a revenue ceiling well below the $100 million mark after years of investment and focused work.

PRM hasn't had its category killer. There is no equivalent to Snowflake in data warehouses, Intuit in finance, Workday in HR tech, or Atlassian in project management. Those companies all reached hundreds of millions in revenue at high growth rates, went public, and saw multibillion-dollar valuations. Yet in PRM, we just don't have an equivalent.

No category-defining company has broken through to large public-scale heights. Why? It's because partner ecosystems haven't broken through to public-scale relevance in how and when they create value for their companies. They're sitting at the kids' table.

Ecosystem-led growth fundamentally changes this paradigm, and it does so by solving the "partner paradox"—let's tackle that next.

5

Why Legacy Partnerships Were Set Up to Fail

Now that we know more about the old world of legacy partnerships and the technologies that power them, we can explore the reasons they often fall short. This sets the stage for ecosystem-led growth as a way forward, elevating the practice of partnership building and allowing partner ecosystems to make a more clear and direct impact on the way companies grow.

Every year since 2020, Crossbeam has published the results of a comprehensive survey of the partnership industry called "**The State of the Partner Ecosystem**" (SOPE). Every year we've seen the same incredible result: partnership professionals are absolutely certain that their work delivers undeniable growth, leverage, and value to their companies. And the same overwhelming majority of professionals report that their departments are underfunded and underappreciated by the companies they work for (see Figure 5.1).

What gives?

We've seen this enough that we have a name for it: the **partnership paradox**. How is it that a growth function inside of a company can be such an important source of revenue growth and yet also be so universally unfundable?

I saw this issue for 15 years working in SaaS before Crossbeam, and I'm embarrassed to say that I was one of the many CEOs who underfunded

FIGURE 5.1 The partner paradox: How can both be true?

partnerships myself. My reason was actually quite straightforward, as harsh as it is to say out loud:

- Due to a lack of data and **attribution**, I didn't have conviction that the partner teams were actually making the impact they thought they were.
- Due to a lack of scalable playbooks and systems, I didn't believe that giving them more money would result in proportionally more results.

Sorry, partner people. When you find yourself in the partnership paradox, these are the things that your CEO is thinking but may not have the heart to say out loud.

Historically, partnerships are kept around not because of what they deliver by existing but because of the fear of what would happen if they did not exist at all. Partner teams are "glue people" that string together value stories across sales, marketing, and product but don't necessarily own any of that upside individually and directly. Worse yet, they're totally blind to the positive impact they make for their partners because the data needed to show that impact is out of their reach.

As a result, partner teams slip into being something wholly unscalable: a human-powered trust layer. Via human interactions and conversations, rapport is built, trust is established, access is granted, and collaboration grows.

This is where all the negative connotations of partnerships come from in the modern tech economy. The "hugs and chugs" event interactions, the title inflation for displaced founders and sales leaders, the partnership paradox in general. Humans with the relationship capital to inspire and convey trust are leveraged as the "glue" to hold together alliances between businesses where there is otherwise no protocol for collaboration. It doesn't scale; you can't measure it, but everyone can feel in their bones the incredible value that it brings.

So these partnership workers are kept in a holding pattern of believing in their value, getting patted on the head from time to time, but when scrutinized quantitatively they're left looking as if they're all sizzle and no steak.

This is the world of partnerships I witnessed at my previous companies, the source of skeptical reactions I got from venture capitalists (VCs) when talking about making partnership hires, and the origin story of the partnership paradox.

But why? The answer goes all the way back to the first principles of how to build a business, grounded in mathematics and game theory.

It's clear that partnership collaboration has unique properties. After all, in other areas of business, we don't need "human glue" to establish trust. Okta can manage our logins through code, Zapier can traffic our most sensitive data through authentication schemes, and ADP can store our salaries and bank accounts as a matter of day-to-day business. So why are partnerships so different?

The answer is actually quite simple. In all those other examples, the data involved is wholly and exclusively the property of your company. It's the logins of your users to your systems. It's the amount your business pays to your employees. It's the movement of your data between your company's applications for your company's use.

In partnerships, nearly all the most pertinent questions you seek to answer involve breaking down the silos of data between one or more companies.

Consider perhaps the three most simple and fundamental questions at hand in most partner collaborations:

1. How many customers do we have in common, and who are they?
2. Are my sales reps currently selling to any of the same companies as your sales reps?
3. Which companies in my target market do you know that I don't, and how can you help me connect with them?

Whether it's a channel partner, tech partner, or strategic partner, the answers to these questions might unlock an infinite stream of actions, collaborations, and value creation between you and them. If answered, the results could constitute an always-refreshing, actionable "data layer" that could sit at the heart of your collaboration.

But throughout the long course of business history, these simple questions have been largely unanswerable.

Look back at the huge list of PRM features from Chapter 4. Not a single one of them directly solves for these questions. Instead, you get a universe of features that help companies get at the answers through approximations, strategies that circumvent the core questions at hand, or allow for the one-directional passage and control of the knowledge one deal at a time.

The closest thing you get is lead registration, a technique by which one party fills out a form to share individual lead activity with another without any context on how that lead might intersect with the receiving party's existing **sales pipeline**.

The reason this data is missing boils down to basic math—set theory to be exact. You cannot answer these basic questions without drawing a Venn diagram between your **data silo** (that is, your sales pipeline and other CRM data) and your partner's data silo (see Figure 5.2).

But Venn diagrams have a fatal flaw: you cannot determine what sits "in the middle" of a Venn diagram without first having full access to all of the data in both of the input sets.

Practically speaking, that means that I can't know where my customer base overlaps with yours unless you give me the complete list of all your customers (or I give you mine). For a whole host of strategic, legal, and privacy-related reasons, this is not a tenable strategy for any serious company.

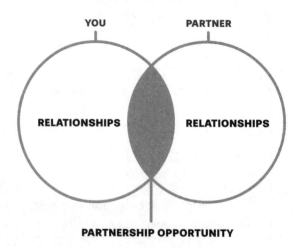

FIGURE 5.2 The data Venn diagram.

If you've ever taken a game theory class or gone down the right You-Tube rabbit hole, you may recognize this as the **prisoner's dilemma**. It's a game theory thought experiment dating back to scientists Merrill Flood and Melvin Dresher in the 1950s.

The model goes like this: You've just been arrested for bank robbery. Across a dark hallway, your accomplice Richard is being led into a conference room. As the door slams shut, police begin questioning him. Your hands shake. Your body quivers. Most of all, your mind races.

What is Richard telling the police? Is he blaming the robbery on me? Would he stay loyal to me in the face of serious prison time?

Your mind races even more. You weigh your options and the outcomes.

What should I say when I'm questioned? Should I defect and implicate Richard or try to cooperate with my accomplice and stay silent?

You and Richard are stuck in the prisoner's dilemma. Your outcomes will depend on how you and Richard each behave (see Figure 5.3).

The best overall outcome (two years of prison each) is attainable only if both of you stay silent, but you have no way of ensuring that the other will do so. Even though you both have every reason to trust each other, the risk of being defected on is so great that it makes you wonder if cooperating

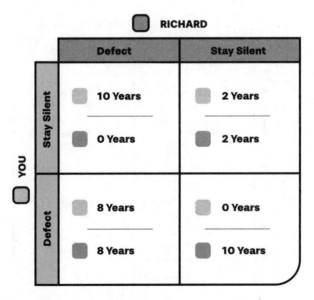

FIGURE 5.3 The prisoner's dilemma.

with Richard is the right move. Complicating things is the fact that he's surely doing the same math.

What would you do in that situation? Well, game theory does give us a "correct" answer—known as the **Nash equilibrium**—and it's a chilling one: always defect. Even though mutual cooperation leads to a better overall outcome, the game is rigged against you. Each individual always fares better if they defect, regardless of what the other person does.

Ironically, this leads to the worst outcome always taking place: both sides defect. You can each kiss eight years goodbye.

That feeling of dread may feel familiar. Let's take the prisoner's dilemma model and change the stakes from jails to sales. Whew. Imagine that you and your partner are deciding if it's worth answering the question "How many sales opportunities do we have in common?"

Rather than a prison sentence (downside risk), it's now about the upside of your collaboration (shared wins). And rather than ratting out your co-conspirator, your decision is whether or not to share your sales pipeline data with an otherwise trusted partner. It's the same game (see Figure 5.4).

Unfortunately, the Nash equilibrium is also the same. Every company, every time chooses to "defect" (in this case, not sharing any data). Their partners do too. So these "defects" not only limit the efficiency of

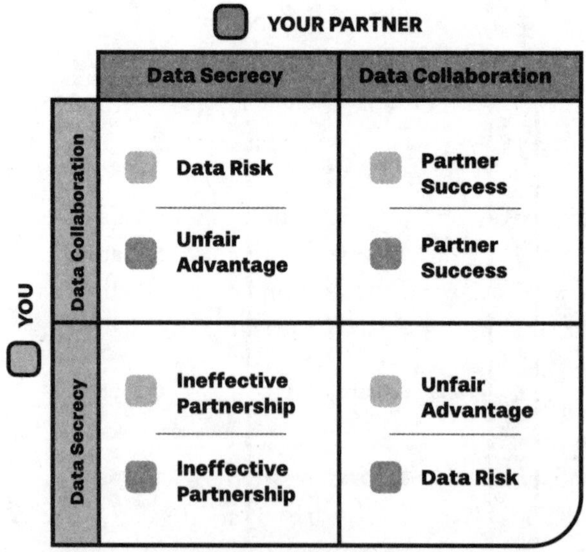

FIGURE 5.4 The partnership dilemma.

partnerships themselves (and the success of the parties involved in them), but they also limit the overall value brought to the market via partners working together, so in aggregate, a lot of market value is lost.

Without a way to break down the data silos between companies, there is no core data asset on which to build a growth platform between your companies. Think about it: sales SaaS is all built on CRM data, marketing SaaS is built on your contact lists, finance SaaS is built on your accounting books, and human resources SaaS is built on your employee data. This is how the emergence of a SaaS platform happens: an organized new data asset emerges, and an economy of applications is built on top of it.

The partnerships industry hasn't been transformed by modern software because it doesn't yet have a data layer that spans all partners and is trusted by all partners. The physics of the prisoner's dilemma have kept that data layer locked up while so many other categories could emerge on top of more tightly controlled silos of your own data that aren't subject to these constraints.

Through this lens, it's understandable why the behaviors of partner teams have always fallen back to the anti-patterns we've seen in the world of partnerships:

- *Humans as glue:* Major decisions around priorities, partner selection, actions to take, and performance measurement fall on manual actions and discretion from human beings.
- *Async account mapping:* Without a software platform to govern collaboration, partnership professionals go "under the radar" and email spreadsheets of hand-curated raw CRM data between themselves and their partners to see where the overlaps are. Usually this takes days and involves using a lot of wonky spreadsheet formulas like VLOOKUP that help users piece together where and how datasets might match. This is often an unknown "shadow" practice that hides from the purview of legal and security teams and is chronically flawed due to data age and completeness issues, measurement challenges, and security risks. But it's everywhere.
- *PRM as core tech:* Partner teams spend what little budget they have on systems that help automate and scale the flawed playbooks. Rather than collaborating with partners, more focus exists on onboarding, educating, and scoring them based on one-directional and imperfect streams of leads. The vast majority of partners are ROI-negative, and success rates are impossible to predict.

And this is where I found myself a few years back, on the heels of selling Stitch Data and after a decade-long journey of navigating the prisoner's dilemma problem with RJMetrics and its acquirers.

It was clear that the way in which companies scaled through their partner ecosystems was in desperate need of playbooks that matched the opportunity at hand. The industry needed a catalyst on which to build these playbooks. It needed a solution to the prisoner's dilemma of partnerships and a foundation on which a generation of better technology solutions could be built.

It needed an ecosystem data layer.

6 The Ecosystem Data Layer Arrives

In 2016, we sold RJMetrics to Magento, and I joined their in-house growth and strategy team for 18 months as part of the deal. Magento was over 10 times our size, and it was there that I got my first peek at how big companies build ecosystems and leverage their partnerships for growth.

Surely, I speculated, there must be some solution for the prisoner's dilemma collaboration issues I had encountered in my past. I couldn't wait to see it.

To my surprise, there was no solution. I saw the same issues from my past—just 10 times larger. The prisoner's dilemma plagued partner strategy at a radically larger scale, across an ecosystem that included hundreds of tech partners and tens of thousands of channel partners.

It turned out that there wasn't some magical reason why this problem goes away when you get big. There's not some module you can pay Salesforce a million dollars to unlock that suddenly lets you compare and cross-pollinate data across silos at scale. All I saw were the same anti-patterns: human glue, emailed spreadsheets, and legacy PRM.

If the goal of a start-up entrepreneur is to discover pockets of potential product-market fit, I certainly felt like I'd stumbled upon the "market" side—solving the prisoner's dilemma at scale across modern partner ecosystems might just unlock a multibillion-dollar opportunity.

Of course, the "product" side of product-market fit was still elusive. That is, until we started building my second company, Stitch Data.

There, I saw the API economy exploding in scale and the very nature of partnerships evolving into a core, strategic driver of modern company strategy. I saw a new generation of companies being built on the premise that modern APIs allow you to move and transform data at a scale and level of security never before seen. And it all clicked.

What if we used the modern data stack and the modern API economy to build something new that was specifically designed to solve the prisoner's dilemma problem in partner ecosystems?

It would act like an escrow service for data: a secure, independent third party that sits in between companies that want to collaborate with each other and handles the technical and privacy complexities at the heart of the prisoner's dilemma problem. It could receive data from both sides and only expose the discreet insights found at the intersection of those datasets, all while making sure each side retains ownership and control of its data.

And it could take care of all the hard parts:

- Technology to extract, transform, and load (ETL) data from your company's systems of record (that is, CRM);
- A universal data model into which all data could be mapped, allowing datasets to be compared across company lines even if the companies involved used different CRMs or organized their sales pipelines differently;
- An identity resolution layer to ensure that "a match is a true match" even when confusing names and data structures exist; and
- A trust, privacy, and security layer that allows each company to independently manage and control who sees what data under what circumstances, down to each individual field and each individual partner.

This was the "product" piece, right before our eyes. It would have been impossible just five years in the past due to the immaturity of the API economy, and five years in the future it might just be too late. It was now or never. It was Crossbeam.

We launched in 2019.

If successful, Crossbeam would facilitate a network of interconnected companies all using it to securely and thoughtfully define the surface area of their collaborations within their ecosystems.

This, at long last, would lead to the emergence of the missing partner ecosystem data layer.

Every company would go from having a singular, siloed view of their accounts to a multi-CRM view that contained not just their knowledge about companies from their own data silo but also all of the combined knowledge about those companies that every partner in their ecosystem was willing to share. All updated automatically, curated to fit your use cases, and delivered to the fingertips of your teams in the field.

On top of that data layer, an entire economy of applications could emerge. These would finally allow partner ecosystems to be scaled, actioned, and measured through a whole new growth playbook that meets the needs of our time and doesn't suffer the inherent flaws of those that came before it.

We launched in 2019, and the following few years were unlike anything I had experienced in my career. I'd seen glimpses of product-market fit in my past companies, some stronger than others, but this was unique.

We quickly learned that network effects would be both the gift and the curse of our business. What we had stumbled on was one of just a few of its kind in the world: a true B2B network graph.

This graph would not be a social network like LinkedIn because the connections are between companies, not people. It also isn't a marketplace network graph, because there aren't buyers and sellers or some other dynamic. And its value was much more than just "data network effects" where SaaS companies roll up user data to improve their product—no, the graph itself is the value proposition of our product.

As a result, we soon faced the infamous **cold start problem** outlined by Andrew Chen in his eponymous 2022 book. Cold start problems in network businesses can kill such companies before they even start—they are the chicken-and-egg resulting from the fact that networks grow when value is being delivered, but value can only be delivered via the network.

Our solve at Crossbeam, quite frankly, was to spend every last ounce of relationship capital I'd built up in the past decade as a founder. At our launch in January 2019, I called up my closest friends and contacts and convinced them to join.

A total of eight of them did, and Figure 6.1 shows what our network graph looked like in January 2019.

Each dot is a company that registered, and each line connecting those companies is a partnership between them. That first partnership shown is between my recently acquired former company Stitch Data and its close partner Looker.

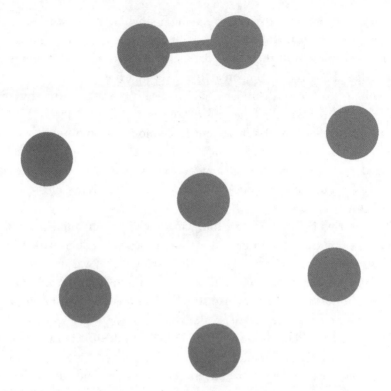

FIGURE 6.1 Crossbeam network graph, January 2019.

Yes, that's right, the very company that defeated my first start-up to the tune of a $2.6 billion exit was also the first company to help us break through the cold start problem here at Crossbeam. I'm eternally grateful to Keenan Rice and my foes-turned-friends on the Looker founding team.

Within a year, as I further pounded my contacts list, we started to see a secondary source of new signups: our existing users. By January 2020, just a year later, we were seeing more new companies sign up because they were invited onto the platform by users other than the ones signing up because they were pitched into it by yours truly (see Figure 6.2).

Note how a "mesh" forms over time, as opposed to a universe of individual hub-and-spoke constellations. Even when a "supernode" company has a large number of partners, connections also form between those partners, which increases the density of the graph overall.

It was at this point we started measuring what is called the *k-factor*. Sometimes referred to as the *virality coefficient*, the **k-factor** measures one

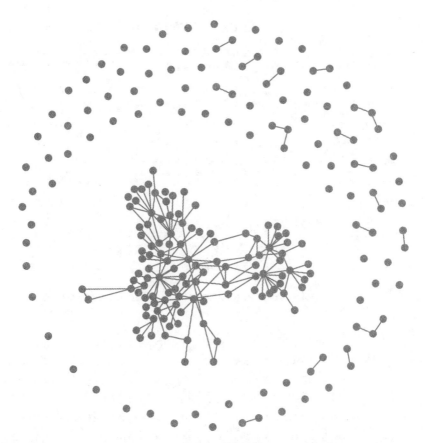

FIGURE 6.2 Crossbeam network graph, January 2020.

thing: for any new member of the network, what is the average number of additional members they will be responsible for adding? On a B2B network graph, a "member" is a company.

The k-factor metric is incredibly powerful. At any value greater than 1.0 (meaning each new member will invite exactly one more new member), the network growth is inherently exponential in nature. As others have observed in the past, even a low k-factor can be a powerful growth multiplier.

At Crossbeam, the nature of our platform naturally led users to invite their partners. While we may have signed them up in pairs initially, once the value was demonstrated with one partner, it wasn't uncommon for users to invite their entire ecosystems onboard.

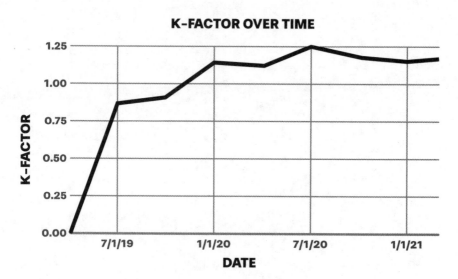

FIGURE 6.3 Crossbeam's k-factor during initial network surge.

We watched our k-factor climb quickly in those first two years and sta-bilize north of 1.0 throughout 2020, leading to an explosive year of growth in our network and overall adoption (see Figure 6.3). It was the latest in a long line of market signals: ELG was arriving and quickly.

The COVID-19 pandemic destroyed the events economy, a mainstay of where the in-person, data-starved approach to partner management had thrived. It's hard to do "hugs and chugs" when physical contact is discour-aged and all the bars are closed. We were a superior alternative, forced into widespread awareness by the absence of legacy options.

A strange truth about growing Crossbeam in 2020 is the morbid correla-tion between what we were trying to create at our company and what the world was working to stop at the same time: viral growth.

The math behind calculating k-factor for our network and measuring the viral spread of COVID-19 was, quite uncomfortably, identical. Our wonky growth hacking metric had suddenly become a topic of mainstream discussion and armchair analysis. In turn, it felt kind of gross to celebrate "virality" and showcase exponential growth charts in this era. But at this point, the network seemed to gain a mind of its own, and even our unease couldn't slow down what was to come.

By January 2021, our network had grown to 2,000 organizations, up from just eight exactly two years before (see Figure 6.4). At this point,

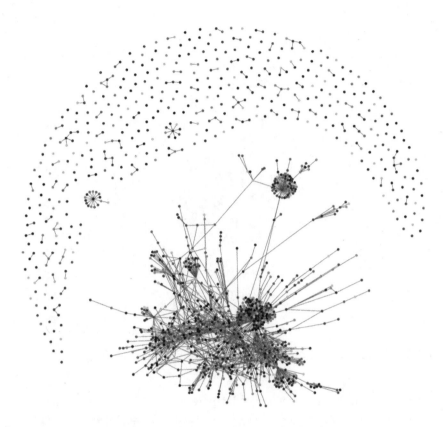

FIGURE 6.4 Crossbeam network graph, January 2021.

our North Star changed from solving the "cold start" problem to providing our customers with useful, actionable applications for the data from our network.

But the network didn't stop. By 2023, it had crossed 15,000 companies including 90% of the Forbes Cloud 100 of best private tech companies, 86% of the Bessemer Emerging Cloud Index of public tech companies, and over a thousand companies north of $100 million of annual revenue (see Figure 6.5).

We'd be foolish to think that this growth was just because of a good idea or a well-built product. This kind of adoption curve also requires a healthy dose of good timing and incredible luck.

As it turns out, those factors were abundantly present for us at Crossbeam. While we had our heads buried in network effects, k-factor, and

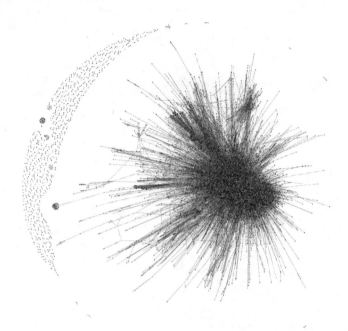

FIGURE 6.5 Crossbeam network graph, September 2023.

the lingo of the partnerships world, the world around us was undergoing a disruptive set of changes. These changes would open a door for ELG to resonate more powerfully and rapidly than we could have ever engineered on our own. It would also leave a generation of legacy growth playbooks in its wake.

7

Why Now? The Disruption of Growth as We Know It

The success of a business movement such as ecosystem-led growth doesn't just hinge on good ideas—it also requires good timing. A major reason why ELG is having its moment is because the sun is setting on a deep bench of growth strategies that just don't work like they used to.

Artificial intelligence (AI) is having a transformative impact on everything we know about how companies are built and run. We're in the most complex and fraught regulatory environment that we've ever seen. A volatile tech economy has put valuations onto a roller coaster that requires an incredible agility in how trade-offs are made between growth and efficiency.

In the midst of this rapidly changing environment, many companies have found themselves as part of an equation where the old numbers no longer balance. Companies everywhere are scrambling for new growth paradigms as the old playbooks let them down.

Ecosystem-led growth is the shining star in this galaxy of expanding darkness.

In this chapter, we'll dive into the shifts that have hit the innovation economy in recent history and how the playbooks of my past have all become collateral damage, one by one.

Inbound Marketing and the Great AI Reset

I love inbound marketing. Throughout my career, it has been my go-to-market love language and at the heart of some of my most successful work as a founder and growth engineer. But change is afoot, and the traditional inbound marketer is at risk of going the way of the VCR repair man.

Inbound marketing is a strategy that focuses on attracting customers through valuable and relevant content. The category first emerged in the early 2000s, when marketing pioneers Brian Halligan and Dharmesh Shah, cofounders of HubSpot, recognized that many prospective customers were seeking out information on their own terms, turning to the Internet to find answers to their questions and solutions to their problems.

Inbound marketing encompasses a variety of techniques, including content marketing, search engine optimization (SEO), social media marketing, email marketing, and more. Through these channels, companies create and distribute valuable, educational, and engaging content that addresses the needs of their target audience. That audience seeks out the content and arrives at their website from the outside-in, hence the term *inbound*.

One of the key reasons inbound marketing has been widely embraced by B2B companies is that it aligns well with the complex and lengthy buying process typical of B2B transactions. By creating high-quality content and optimizing it for search engines and social media, businesses generate organic traffic and leads over time. This approach is not only more sustainable (you write something once, and it can deliver traffic for years) but also tends to yield better results, as inbound leads are often more qualified and have a higher **conversion rate**.

The inbound playbook all starts with some form of **content marketing**. This is the technique where businesses generate valuable content to attract, engage, and ultimately convert their target audience. By offering informative and relevant content, companies establish themselves as thought leaders in their respective industries and build trust with potential and existing customers.

That is, until now. The advent of **generative AI**, specifically ChatGPT and its incredible ecosystem of integrations, is showing signs of rapidly changing the landscape of inbound marketing. **ChatGPT is a large language model (LLM)**, which has been trained on vast amounts of text data, resulting in an unprecedented ability to interpret data and generate results.

In other words, it can write, from prose to code, in every language. It can generate images. It can take feedback and iterate on results. And it's good—but at the same time disruptive.

Brian Halligan, the cofounder of HubSpot, remarked on *The Logan Bartlett Show* in March 2023 that he thought ChatGPT "is a disruptive innovation. AWS was a disruptive innovation that led to a million SaaS companies. The iPhone was a disruptive innovation that led to so many mobile applications. I think this is similar."

AI-powered language models such as ChatGPT have made it possible to generate vast quantities of high-quality content at an unprecedented speed. This has flooded the market with content, making it increasingly challenging to stand out in a saturated space. Consequently, the returns on investment from content marketing efforts have diminished, as it has become harder to capture the attention of the target audience.

You may think this doesn't apply to you—perhaps your market is too bespoke, and a generative AI model couldn't possibly opine on it with authority. I would encourage you to check your ego. When I look back on the inbound marketing strategies that have worked for me at past companies, I am humbled at just how antiquated they sound in today's AI landscape.

Here's a quick example: back at Stitch, we built an incredibly successful SEO strategy based on dynamically generated long-tail content about how to move data from SaaS tools into data warehouses. It was actually a pretty clever hack: we did some basic research to assemble and write content about "how to extract data from X" and "how to load data into Y" (where X was one of a hundred or so popular SaaS solutions, and Y was one of a few dozen data warehouses or analytics tools).

Then we built a web application that dynamically generated a unique website for every possible combination of X and Y. The result was hundreds of web pages such as "Exporting MailChimp data to Redshift" or "Exporting HubSpot data to Snowflake," each of which was a spot-on answer to an extremely specific search that might be conducted by someone in our target market.

Of course, at the end of each page was a simple call to action about how it's much easier to just have Stitch do all this heavy lifting for you. People searching for those terms were highly qualified for our product by definition, and we had the only site page on the Internet that lined up perfectly with their query.

To Google's algorithms, these web pages gave useful bespoke instructions for piping data from a specific SaaS tool into a specific destination. We became the top result for searches such as "Salesforce to Snowflake," even outranking the documentation pages from those companies themselves (see Figure 7.1).

This was a long-tail strategy. While any given individual page may have received only one or two visits a day, in aggregate this inbound marketing play drove thousands of highly qualified leads to Stitch each month and was the number two source of revenue for the business (after our partner ecosystem, of course).

Back then I was able to pull this off only because I possessed a deep understanding of APIs, a willingness to get my hands dirty with days and days of research, a knack for distilling technical concepts into human-readable prose, and enough programming knowledge to design a web server that dynamically stitched together disparate pieces of my content based on the URL it was serving.

Fast-forward to today. Who needs a database or a clever algorithm for stitching up content? If I wanted to generate hundreds of long-tail search

FIGURE 7.1 A Stitch "X to Y" SEO page, ca. 2018.

pages that combine easily researched API documentation based on a list of sources and destinations, an intern could do it in an afternoon using Chat-GPT prompts. Heck, they could probably generate thousands of pages, not hundreds. And when they were done, ChatGPT could walk them through setting up the hosting for the sites as well.

AI has transformed some of my best ideas into huge wastes of human time. As this example shows, we are experiencing a highly disruptive, industry-redefining wave of changes for content marketing strategy as we know it, fundamentally disrupting the way companies gain key advantages as part of their inbound marketing strategies.

I can hear the arguments already: Quality over quantity! Creativity still matters! AI can't come up with new ideas! Just wait.

People underestimate the power of these models and overestimate the creativity required to create long-tail content that is indistinguishable from that generated by most content marketers. Also, this tech is in its relative infancy and only getting smarter by the day.

I can remember a time when people said, "AI may take away jobs from the chess players, engineers, and mathematicians, but it will never create art." For many, it was long assumed that creative endeavors such as writing and the visual arts would be the hardest nut for AI to crack. We were wrong. It came for the creatives first, and, damn, is it getting good fast.

As an author, I've gotten advice to not include anything in my book that will date it and make it seem old or antiquated too fast. I'm really rolling the dice with this one, but I feel the need to admit that I'm sitting here in 2024 at publication time and this technology is absolutely blowing my mind. Yet within a year or two, marketers will view it as commonplace. Creative, content, and inbound marketing are undergoing a once-in-a-lifetime disruption.

By way of example, I just opened up the AI image generator Midjourney and sent the simple prompt "photo of two excited business people, one looking at the other one's laptop screen and making some kind of exciting discovery about a joint business opportunity. Photorealistic, black and white." Thirty seconds later I had the photograph shown in Figure 7.2.

Just fathom the expense and time that would have been spent generating an image like this in the past. Actors, contracts, lighting, lenses, postproduction, and so on.

A key to appreciating this evolution is to admit that most talents, including those in the creative space, are distributed along a **power law curve**.

FIGURE 7.2 B&W photograph generated by the author via Midjourney.

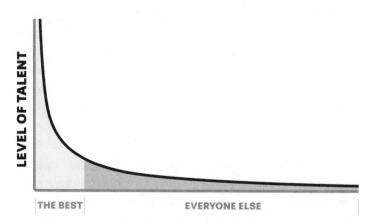

FIGURE 7.3 The long tail of talent quality.

The top 1% of creators and writers aren't just 10x better than the top 10%, they're hundreds or even thousands of times better (see Figure 7.3).

For your typical B2B company, the chances that you have a top 1% content creator or visual designer on staff is statistically miniscule. But the emergence of these AI tools are already better than the creators in the bottom 50%, and I would argue that they can take a "top 50%" creative and supercharge their work product and efficiency such that they are indistinguishable from someone in the top 10%. AI hasn't yet toppled the top 1% yet in my book, but it's coming for them.

In the coming years, therefore, this isn't necessarily a job destroyer so much as it is a force multiplier. It will make content creators faster and more prolific. This will lead to the same zero-sum, market-flooding effects we saw inside of people's inboxes when outbound email automation went mainstream. Only now it's coming for your search engine results page (SERP). To Halligan's point, this is disruptive innovation happening right before our eyes.

Which brings us to the next falling domino in inbound marketing: **search engine optimization (SEO)**. SEO is the practice of optimizing websites and content to improve their visibility on search engines such as Google. By targeting specific keywords and implementing various on-page and off-page techniques, businesses increase their organic search rankings and drive more traffic to their websites.

You can probably see where this is going.

Historically, SEO—especially long-tail SEO used by many inbound marketing practitioners to target highly specific keywords—has been an effective strategy due to the limited competition and the manual nature of content creation and optimization. However, with AI-generated content flooding the market, SEO suffers from a one-two punch of diminishing returns.

First, when the bar for creating new content drops to near zero, the rate at which the Internet will be inundated with search-optimized content is unfathomable. AI-based tools can now analyze, optimize, and even predict search engine algorithms, making it increasingly difficult for businesses to maintain their edge or for the "good guys to win" by creating a small focused library of human-generated content.

The decades-long cat-and-mouse game between Google and thousands of eager SEO experts seeking to game the results is over. The SEO experts have AI now. Google as we know it has lost this cat-and-mouse game, becoming a Tom to AI's Jerry.

Second, and perhaps more damning over the long term, AI itself may be the most viable threat to traditional search engines as we know them. In a world where chat interfaces can provide direct, refined, and accurate answers to even the most complex questions, many are arguing that the clock has started on traditional query-based web searches going the way of dial-up Internet. A fast, reliable answer is a step function improvement over clicking through a handful of ad-ridden search engine links.

Organic search traffic is a critical path for the success of many inbound marketing strategies, again undermining the long-term viability of this playbook.

As with outbound marketing, we can already see traditional inbound tactics evolving from a "dark arts" differentiator for early adopters into a noise machine that floods its channel with middling content. The result is a less effective channel for all, as even the best practitioners must overinvest to separate themselves from the noise.

Outbound Sales: A Negative-Sum Game

Most mainstream business advice gets served up to entrepreneurs ad nauseam through viral tweets, well-intentioned advisors, and overhyped business books (uh oh). Sometimes, however, there's an idea so valuable that it only gets talked about in private rooms and passed from founder to founder with the secrecy of nuclear launch codes.

That's how I felt when one of my RJMetrics board members told me to read the book *Predictable Revenue* by Aaron Ross back in 2011 (see Figure 7.4). With a wink and a nod, I was "in the know" about how the fastest-growing tech companies were supercharging their growth. The book was thin, more pamphlet than textbook, and had a homemade feel to it. But what it contained was a growth playbook that would define an era.

In the book, Ross details the techniques he used as an early leader at Salesforce.com to generate a seemingly endless flow of sales leads and meetings for account executives. The secret? Eye-catching, hand-written cold emails that landed directly in the inboxes of Salesforce's top prospects. Ross advocated for putting down the phone and instead focusing on the inbox. He called for companies to do this at scale, in high volumes, and using dedicated team members called **sales development representatives (SDRs)**.

This may sound too obvious to warrant a whole book, but at the time it was revolutionary. Cold-calling was overdone yet still the norm in most

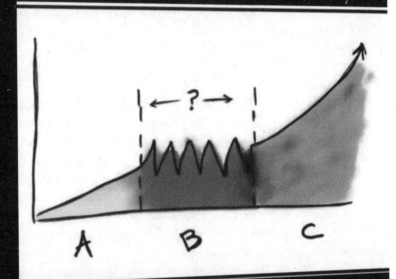

FIGURE 7.4 *Predictable Revenue.*

outbound selling circles, and many senior execs at big companies were only then finally catching up to using email as their primary channel of communication. This was a clear "why now" moment for cold email outreach.

Within a few years, the modern SDR role was commonplace as companies across the globe flocked to create email-based outbound teams to fuel their growth. Software solutions, most notably Outreach and SalesLoft, were launched specifically to automate and scale this technique.

The initial allure of outbound selling was that it promised a systematic, predictable way to generate leads and increase revenue. In these early days, outbound SDR teams enjoyed high response rates and conversion rates, thanks to relatively low competition and the novelty factor of their approach. However, as the technique proliferated, it began to lose its edge.

A major contributing factor to the decay in outbound sales efficiency is the sheer volume of cold emails flooding business inboxes. This deluge of messages has led to "inbox fatigue," with recipients becoming increasingly discerning and selective about the emails they open and engage with.

There has also been a separate innovation working against these strategies and tools. Advanced spam filters and email security measures have become increasingly adept at identifying and blocking unsolicited emails, making it more difficult for cold emails to reach their intended recipients.

But wait, there's more! Tightening data privacy regulations, such as the European Union's **General Data Protection Regulation (GDPR)** and the **California Consumer Privacy Act (CCPA)**, have called the legality of these approaches into question more categorically.

By the early 2020s, SDR teams were systematically underperforming. In their State of Sales Development Survey, a community of revenue leaders named Pavilion revealed that 73% of SDR teams were under quota between January and September of 2022 (see Figure 7.5).

The diminishing effectiveness of an outbound email strategy has been exacerbated by the fact that SDRs and the software solutions that support them have become more expensive than ever. Pavilion's report showed that the most common on-target earnings (OTE) range for an SDR in the United States is $80,000 to $90,000, with additional costs for benefits and training (see Figure 7.6).

Moreover, the cost of implementing and maintaining sophisticated sales automation software can run into tens of thousands of dollars per year. When considering the low response rates and diminishing returns

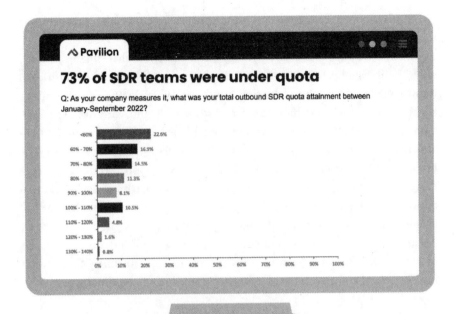

FIGURE 7.5 Pavilion State of Sales Development Survey, fall 2022.

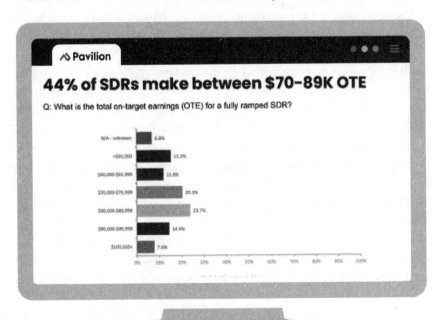

FIGURE 7.6 On-target earnings for sales development representatives.

on investment, it becomes clear that the outbound sales equation no longer balances.

The impact of generative AI tools such as ChatGPT also can't be ignored here. At first glance, these tools will likely be viewed as a force multiplier that could increase the productivity and success of SDRs by customizing and personalizing their messaging at high speeds and volumes. The end-game is less clear, however, as it will inevitably lead to higher email volumes and further dilute the efficacy of any given message that hits a zero-sum inbox. Add in AI solutions that read your inbox for you and filter out sales messages before you see them, and you get a "bots battling bots" effect that neutralizes effectiveness even further. One way or another, the days of free lunches and easy wins through outbound selling are over.

In short, costs are up, and effectiveness is down. In under a decade, this secret weapon evolved from a lucrative arbitrage opportunity to a money pit. Any company still leaning hard on this strategy is holding the bag.

A Targeted Attack on Targeted Ads

In the early days of the digital age, online advertising emerged as a highly effective and promising source of growth for B2B companies. However, the effectiveness of online advertising was challenged when Apple introduced its "Ask App Not to Track" functionality in Spring 2021. This feature has prevented apps deployed on iOS from tracking users without their explicit consent, thereby degrading the quality of targeting capabilities. The move was a response to growing concerns about privacy and data protection, and it set the stage for a significant shift in the digital advertising landscape.

Surprise, surprise: when prompted, consumers don't like to be tracked. Analytics company Flurry observed opt-in rates to tracking in the United States hovering below 20% in the months following Apple's change (see Figure 7.7).

As more users began to adopt this feature, B2B advertisers found it more difficult to obtain the granular data required to deliver targeted ads. Yet, they keep spending—ad revenues haven't seen a material decline. The result is sustained prices despite compromised quality, which directly ripples through to the return-on-investment math for digital ads.

Around the same time, the introduction of the GDPR in the European Union and the CCPA in the United States further limited the extent to

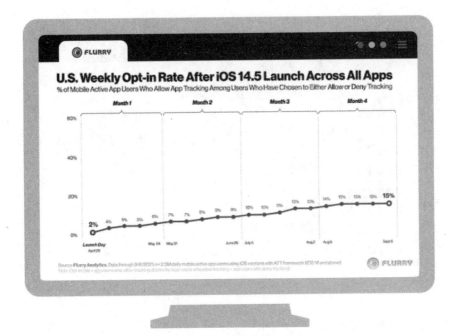

FIGURE 7.7   News flash: no one opts into tracking.

which individuals could be tracked and targeted by advertisers. These regulations enforced strict data privacy and protection standards, in most cases requiring companies to obtain explicit user consent before collecting and processing personal information (see Figure 7.8). For B2B advertisers and ad platforms, these regulations meant having to adapt their targeting strategies to comply with new privacy requirements.

Here too, the tracking and enrichment capabilities that allowed for precise tracking and targeting at high volumes have suffered. This accrues even more toward the ROI challenges of targeted online advertising.

What a roller coaster. In less than a decade, the landscape of online advertising has shifted dramatically for B2B companies. What was once a scalable and cost-effective growth lever, seemingly brimming with arbitrage and opportunity, has now become one of the most expensive means of reaching potential customers despite multiple angles of attack on its effectiveness and ROI.

With cash more precious than ever, it's a path that fewer and fewer companies will be willing or able to bet their budget on.

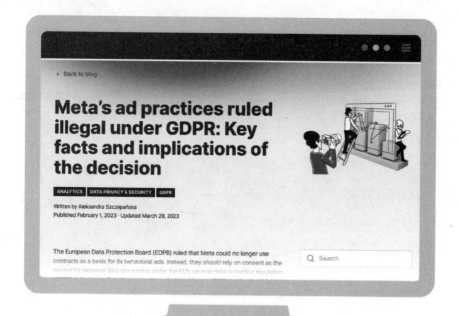

FIGURE 7.8 GDPR affecting the ads industry.

Sales Intelligence: The Bundling Era

Remember that Jim Barksdale quote about how you only make money in business by bundling and unbundling? This is a bundling story.

"Sales intelligence" is a software category that encompasses the many ways that data, technology, and workflows can be used to build a better sales organization. That technology spans data enrichment, call intelligence, pipeline analysis, outbound prospecting, personalization, analytics, and more.

But it all started a decade ago when the once-shady industry of **data brokers** met the exploding distribution channel of **software as a service (SaaS)**.

Back then, when people thought of sales intelligence, they thought of knowing more about prospects by purchasing data about them. They could do this by paying a data broker who amassed giant databases of B2B companies and contacts, reselling them over and over again.

DiscoverOrg, founded in 2007, was a pioneer in the data broker space. Their timing was perfect, as they brought the legacy data broker model to

FIGURE 7.9 DiscoverOrg (now ZoomInfo) home page, March 2013.

the modern Internet, where SaaS subscriptions were the distribution model of choice. DiscoverOrg had a single clear value proposition: it sold a kick-ass database of companies, contacts, and org charts. The product was the data. According to its website in 2013, "DiscoverOrg's data quality is driven by a team of 75+ research analysts who are continuously calling into profiled companies to keep data fresh and actionable for sales and marketing teams" (see Figure 7.9).

Now if you've been following me closely, you'd think things might not end so well for DiscoverOrg. Remember GDPR and CCPA? The advent of AI? The destruction of value when commodity assets and strategies see widespread adoption? How would a company like this possibly survive? Well, by 2022, DiscoverOrg—since rebranded as ZoomInfo—had gone public and grown to over $1 billion in revenue.

How did they do it? Over 15 years of product innovations and acquisitions, ZoomInfo evolved to stay relevant. While data has remained its core differentiator, it is far from a data broker—it's now a software company that offers a single pane of glass for your revenue organization (see Figure 7.10).

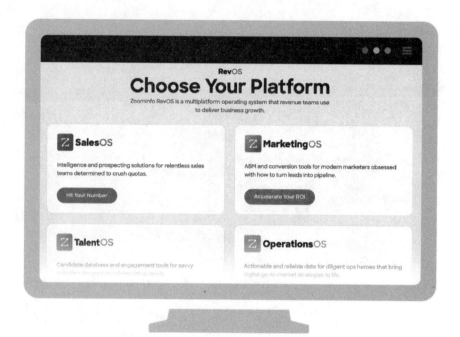

FIGURE 7.10 ZoomInfo home page, April 2023.

ZoomInfo's RevOS is a suite of SaaS tools that now encompasses account-based marketing (ABM), call recording, sales ops—even recruiting! The use of *operating system* as a term for its offering is no mistake. ZoomInfo positions itself as the foundation on which growth solutions are built.

Now that's what I call bundling. ZoomInfo has clearly engaged in a bundling exercise as its product footprint has expanded and entered numerous adjacent micro-categories over the years.

Here's what fascinates me about this space: ZoomInfo's competitive field is packed with other players who have the same story: they pioneered new categories of tech for modern sellers, dominated that category, and then went looking for more addressable market by adding functionality that encroached on the adjacent markets. Eventually, they all just became bundled "sales intelligence" providers vying for the same budget dollars.

Yet no two of these companies started from the same place! What was once a sprawling field of complementary sales tech innovators is now a cutthroat field of post-bundling players in direct competition for the same budget dollars. Let's look at a few of them.

FIGURE 7.11   Clari home page, April 2023.

Clari is a market leader who built its brand on delivering incredible pipeline forecasting solutions. In their own words, today, it's a "revenue platform . . . with solutions for everyone—from reps to execs—you can have full control of your revenue process" (see Figure 7.11). Far more than just forecasting, it offers conversational intelligence, analytics, and data quality features.

Gong, the leader and pioneer in conversation intelligence and revenue intelligence, has built the "revenue intelligence platform" that helps sales teams enhance their most important workflows, including deal execution, coaching, engagement, forecasting, and strategic initiatives.

It's noteworthy that a few years back Gong was in a fight to the death with another player in the call recording space called Chorus.ai—they offered seemingly identical platforms, and their battle accelerated the creation of their category. Whatever became of Chorus? ZoomInfo bought them in July 2021. Bundle-tastic (see Figure 7.12).

Oh, and remember Outreach? The pioneer in outbound sales automation from the "predictable revenue" era? These days they're a "sales

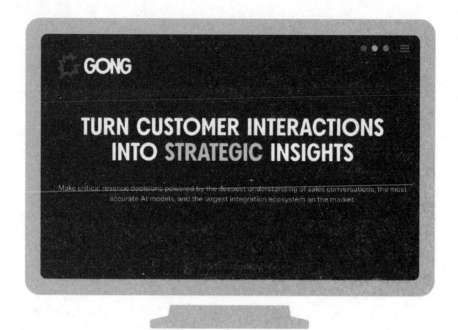

FIGURE 7.12 Gong home page, April 2023.

execution platform" boasting features related to forecasting, conversation intelligence, and deal insights (see Figure 7.13).

Here we have a data broker, a sales forecasting tool, a call recording solution, and an automated outreach tool all moving into each other's product categories and competing head-to-head to be the "single pane of glass" that powers your revenue team.

What does this mean for you, the end company whose business relies on sources of differentiated growth? More category maturity, more convergence, less of an edge. These companies will thrive when one or more become as ubiquitous as CRM—no longer the source of differentiation but instead an essential requirement to operate a sales team.

The bundling evolution in this space serves to reinforce two important points.

First, as these platforms all drift into more horizontal plays, we will see how crucial their partner ecosystems become to carving out a winning position and making them into a true platform. The level of investment in partner ecosystems, APIs, and co-selling in these businesses are skyrocketing across the board.

FIGURE 7.13   Outreach home page, April 2023.

Second, it demonstrates a whole cascade of modern growth techniques that are reaching ubiquity and maturity in its market in tandem, so much so that multiple public or IPO-bound companies are vying for dominance in the space. These days, the chances of being the first company on your block to use these kinds of solutions or finding some arbitrage by adopting what they offer are small. These technologies are now table stakes, more there to keep you competitive than to create long-term differentiation in and of themselves. Where they can provide unique value is in cases where the data and context you feed them is rich and proprietary—and the best source of that grade of data is your partner ecosystem.

Product-Led Growth: A Different Animal

You can hire one SDR. You can test a single ad. You can write a first blog post. But there's no dipping your toe in product-led growth.

Product-led growth (PLG) is a different beast than the growth strategies from the last few chapters. It's not just a tool to drive lead generation, conversion rates, sales cycles, or ACVs. It's an overarching approach to building your company's value proposition that makes those things less relevant.

At its core, PLG is a go-to-market strategy that emphasizes the product itself as the primary driver of business growth. By creating a superior product that delivers immediate and obvious value to users, businesses can attract and retain customers organically, reduce customer acquisition costs, and drive expansion through word-of-mouth referrals and positive reviews.

PLG strategies typically focus on delivering a seamless user experience, fostering user engagement, and providing self-service onboarding and support. Some of the most effective PLG strategies include:

- Freemium models: Offering a free version of the product with limited features to attract users, and then upselling premium features or services to convert them into paying customers (example: Slack);
- Free trials: Allowing potential customers to try the product for a limited time, demonstrating its value and capabilities, and then encouraging them to upgrade to a paid plan (example: Fivetran);
- Viral loops: Designing the product in a way that encourages users to invite others, thereby promoting organic growth through referrals and network effects (example: Airtable); and
- In-product messaging and education: Providing in-app guidance, tutorials, and support resources to help users become proficient with the product, maximizing their likelihood of becoming loyal customers (example: Notion).

We're big adopters and proponents of PLG here at Crossbeam and for good reason. When this stuff works, it *really* works. A world where end users show up, see value, and hand over their credit card sounds like paradise.

Unfortunately, it's rarely that easy. The economics of PLG are lopsided with a lot of up-front investment to build the right product and user experience. The most prolific "overnight success stories" in PLG include businesses that invested years of work to nail their product-market fit and had the patience to sacrifice early stage revenue growth in doing so. PLG isn't for the impatient or the cash-strapped. It's incredible at scale, but that first million is a slog.

Is it any coincidence that PLG methodologies reached the peak of the hype cycle in the midst of the most cash-rich market in our modern history? As competitive VCs gave more and more forward credit for user growth, engagement, and other "leading indicators" of revenue, the methodologies that helped drive these numbers at the expense of early-stage revenue flourished.

It's hard to ignore the fact that so many PLG companies emerged in the early 2020s when so many company-building strategies were later exposed as **zero interest rate phenomena (ZIRP)**. For some companies, I think PLG fits this bill too. When PLG works, it's beautiful—but when up-front cash investments are harder to make, it can become a far more difficult nut to crack. The reality is that it's not a silver bullet for every company, and higher interest rates will have an impact on its relevance to many.

Countless PLG companies that were funded in the 2020–2022 era are in the midst of a rude awakening. These companies need to deliver steep revenue growth in order to catch up to their oversized valuations from frothier times. And they're turning to salespeople to close the gap.

The result? Many PLG companies are finding lower ceilings than they expected and spending more to get there.

Prolific SaaS investor Tomasz Tunguz analyzed this trend in his December 2022 thinkpiece "PLG & Profitability: More Product Doesn't Necessarily Mean Greater Profits." "Surprisingly, PLG companies' profitability has suffered more than sales-led businesses," wrote Tunguz (see Figure 7.14).

He noted some important observations about the weak spots of PLG in his analysis:

- PLG companies' R&D spend hasn't produced new business at the same rate as a dollar invested in sales & marketing after Covid.
- PLG motions tend to focus on smaller businesses, which may be more susceptible to the economic downturn.
- Sales-lead teams cut headcount when account executives don't attain numbers. Engineering teams do this to a lesser extent.
- Software sales cycles have lengthened, which **SLG** companies can mitigate with better sales skills. These longer cycles may reduce the conversion rates of non-sales-assisted PLG motions.
- Some portion of R&D spend should be allocated to customer acquisition cost for all software companies. This should bring PLG sales efficiency closer to SLG figures.
- Management teams ought to be evaluating whether a PLG or SLG investment produces more bookings per dollar invested. The analysis should include customer expansion for several years.

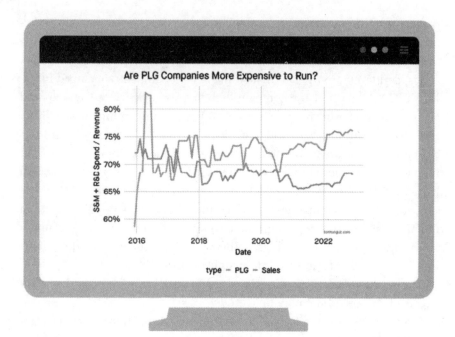

FIGURE 7.14 PLG company operating costs are diverging in the wrong direction.

In today's more rational market, nearly all PLG companies have incorporated traditional salespeople and sales motions into their revenue growth strategies. That means expensive sales reps, compensated by commissions, are driving deals over the finish line. The product may still source some revenue directly and certainly helps fuel the sales pipeline, but when it comes to PLG companies over $10 million of revenue, they all seem to have sales teams. We certainly do at Crossbeam.

This doesn't mean that PLG doesn't work or isn't valuable—it's as awesome as ever in the right hands. But it does introduce quite a few impurities into the utopian growth curves that many founders hope it will bring to their companies.

The messy "PLG sandwich" is found in nearly all PLG companies of scale:

- "PLG" self-serve accounts close at low values and suffer from high churn rates but require no sales touch at all.
- "Sales-assisted" mid-market deals are sourced by the product and PLG motions but require sales or customer service involvement to educate,

procure, and close. It turns out some meaningful subset of business buyers just want to talk to a human at some point.

- "Sales-led" enterprise deals are a mix of product-sourced and sales-sourced in nature and require an enormous amount of sales touch to win and retain. Often these companies can't even sign up for the PLG version of the product due to procurement and IT restrictions.

This sandwich is a sloppy joe, not a BLT. It's messy, and the pieces tend to slop around between the layers as PLG companies find their footing. It requires excellent coordination, and even then, you end up with a stained shirt and having to clean up the scraps with a fork to capture all the goodness.

In this way, PLG isn't a tactic or motion so much as a characteristic of your company's DNA—hard to add, hard to remove, but powerful in conjunction with other techniques.

Another Door Opens

In writing this chapter, I felt like a dinosaur. Everything that made me good at growth strategy over the past 15 years building technology companies seems to have passed its prime.

Founders, operators, and investors have a demonstrated need for something new: a growth strategy that doesn't suffer from the shortfalls of these legacy playbooks.

It must be proprietary in a way that prevents commoditization, even at widespread adoption. It needs to create measurable results and deliver a demonstrably high return on investment.

This is the perfect moment for ecosystem-led growth to emerge. ELG is all these things, showing up in a moment when they are needed most.

Excitingly, ELG also breathes new life back into many of the growth tactics we've learned about in this chapter. Wherever commoditization, inefficiency, regulatory blockers, or general staleness are interfering with a strategy's effectiveness, ELG data can introduce an innovative new lens into who to target, how to message, and the best ways to reach, convert, and retain them as customers.

At long last, let's explore how the ELG phoenix has risen.

It's time for you to claim your place on the graph and begin your company's own ELG journey. We'll begin with the table stakes of setting goals, structuring your team, and overcoming internal objections. From there we'll dive into the playbooks that will make your ELG efforts sing.

PART 3

Beginning Your ELG Journey

Is ELG Right for Me?

Ecosystem-led growth is here, but is this the right moment for your company to adopt it? Let's take a look at a simple framework for assessing your readiness for ELG.

In working with over 15,000 companies at Crossbeam, we've been able to observe businesses at every stage of maturity and every business model. As it turns out, there are two key dimensions that dictate a company's readiness for an ELG strategy: value proposition and company scale.

Value Proposition

Generally speaking, a **value proposition** is the way in which your company delivers value to its customers. As it turns out, the nature of your value proposition is a major input into how well ELG will fit into your business model as a whole.

We're going to think about your value proposition on a spectrum from "stand-alone" to "ecosystem." Companies with **stand-alone value propositions** are extremely independent and deliver value in and of themselves. Some examples would be:

- Your local dine-in pizza place. Go in, eat pizza, head out. There are very few ways that other businesses could be incorporated into the product experience in order to alter or enhance the value proposition to its customers.

- A software development agency that builds new software products for their customers from scratch. They work directly with their customers and build a full deliverable from a blank page with nothing but their own labor.
- My first company, RJMetrics, which we've discussed in detail as a company that chose to build features and hire staff over partnering with outsiders. For the most part, that product had a stand-alone value proposition that didn't require any more than a spreadsheet upload to start delivering value.

On the other extreme of the spectrum are "ecosystem" companies, which would be literally incapable of delivering value if not for other companies that exist in their partner ecosystem. Some examples of **ecosystem value propositions** would be:

- DoorDash, where we find partners galore. From restaurant partners to mobile app store marketplaces to embedded mapping and driver software, it takes a village (rather, an ecosystem) to bring the value proposition of this incredible business to life.
- System integrators, whose entire value proposition is predicated on the sale, implementation, and maintenance of another company's products. No partners, no business.
- My second company, Stitch Data, which was effectively a middleware vendor whose value proposition involved moving data from one partner platform of ours to another. There was no "single player mode" for Stitch: 100% of our customers were in the customer base of at least two of our partners.

The majority of modern tech companies fall on the "ecosystem" side of the spectrum, but there is a big difference between being fully ecosystem dependent and sitting somewhere closer to the middle.

Take Salesforce, the leading provider of CRM software. While their product may seem somewhat stand-alone, few of their customers realize a complete value proposition without implementation help from system integrator partners and installing multiple tech partner integrations from Salesforce's AppExchange marketplace. So which are they? Well, that's why this is a spectrum. I'd put Salesforce on the "ecosystem" side, but not all the way. Most other SaaS tools are the same.

In some pockets of the tech world, this distinction is made between "best of breed" vendors and "suite" vendors. The "best of breed" prioritize assembling the most valuable individual components to create a joint value proposition, while "suite" vendors index on the simplicity of a standalone solution in how they deliver value through a suite of their own features and services.

Company Scale

When companies get big, partner ecosystems become inevitable. Even for companies with strong stand-alone product value propositions, there comes a point where different categories of partners start to become no-brainers.

Channel partners, in particular, become commonplace for companies that are pursuing an international expansion strategy or trying to break into new verticals or user personas. Similarly, working with service partners and marketplaces can be a powerful way to scale your go-to-market efforts when hiring directly presents a scalability or expertise issue.

Scale can also attract technology partner ecosystems even when they've been avoided by design. When you build a large user base there will always be a potential tech partner ecosystem lying in wait, ready to build analytics, workflows, plugins, and other enhancements that augment the value story for your customers—whether you think they need it or not. If you have decent scale and build an API, they will come.

The ELG Readiness Matrix

I love a good 2 × 2 matrix, and I find that they can be a useful way to break down situations like this one where two seemingly independent dimensions come together to answer a hard question. In this case, "Is ELG right for me?" can be answered by looking at the combination of your scale and the extent to which your value proposition is dependent on your partner ecosystem (see Figure 8.1).

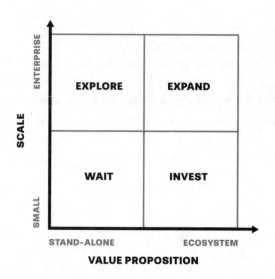

FIGURE 8.1 The ELG readiness matrix.

Placing yourself on this spectrum will likely drop you into one of four distinct quadrants:

- **Small scale, stand-alone value proposition: WAIT.** ELG is probably not for you. The nature of your value proposition means that trying to build an ecosystem just for the sake of running ELG plays with adding partners may be "forcing it." The juice may not be worth the squeeze unless you expand your value proposition or achieve meaningful scale.
- **Small scale, ecosystem value proposition: INVEST.** Companies like these are well suited to invest heavily in ELG, and it may prove to be the most powerful lever they can use to move up the scale dimension of this graph. Their natural connectivity to a partner ecosystem as part of their value proposition means that they are well suited for the playbooks ahead in this book.
- **Enterprise scale, stand-alone value proposition: EXPLORE.** These ones are tricky because they are typically impressive but slower-moving companies who have earned their success by operating in an insular and independent way. However, by not pushing forward with ELG strategies they are almost certainly leaving some amazing growth opportunities on the table. While it may require a crawl, walk, run

approach, companies like these should be doing work to explore ELG and what it could mean for them. If you know an executive at a company in this quadrant, please send them this book!

- **Enterprise scale, ecosystem value proposition: EXPAND.** These are the most fun companies to work with because they most likely have embraced and invested in their ecosystem already, even if the ELG playbooks aren't fully in use within their walls. This means there is opportunity to see outsized returns by taking the inherent value built into their ecosystem and rolling out ELG playbooks at scale. In doing so, they will massively expand both the value created by their ecosystem and likely the ecosystem itself.

If you feel that you're in an awkward middle zone in the graph, you can also consider the rate at which you are moving along these two dimensions to make a call. Do you have a fledgling ecosystem that shows some promise or are you failing to get one off the ground? Are you satisfied at a small scale or working to achieve hypergrowth? Use your directional velocity within this matrix to see where the puck is going, and make the right call on how to proceed.

9

Getting Buy-In for ELG

One of the biggest stumbling blocks faced when rolling out an ecosystem-led growth strategy is failing to earn executive alignment and leadership support. I've seen far too many cases where ambitious and well-intentioned partner teams or sales managers try to "do ELG" on an island at their companies, only to find that they can never quite reach escape velocity or truly solve the partner paradox. Sure, they may create some solid results and strong ROI, but without buy-in outside of their own teams, they never see the kind of trajectory-altering impact that ELG is capable of delivering.

Don't leave ELG sitting at the kids' table.

As we start to explore the core ELG playbooks in the coming chapters, it will become obvious that doing this work in a vacuum is a fool's errand. Every single playbook hinges on cross-functional collaboration, organizational alignment, and a foundation of internal and external trust.

In this chapter we'll explore the most productive avenues for building and securing the support of your entire business.

Setting the Right Goals

If you're playing "business book bingo," this is the part where you might expect me to introduce some new complicated metric or buzzword that helps you measure the success of ELG. It's tempting to do so: that's the kind of fodder that makes for cool graphics and equations, making authors seem innovative and giving them something to sound smart about on podcasts.

Unfortunately for my writing career, however, I'm here to deliver the opposite message: please, please stop making up new metrics.

Perhaps the biggest downfall of traditional partnership teams is that they tend to measure themselves in ways that are poorly understood by everyone else in their companies. Through various mental gymnastics, partner teams tend to justify goals that translate poorly or confusingly into the **key performance indicators** (**KPIs**) of their go-to-market teams and businesses as a whole.

"Has anyone here ever heard of a BIP?" asked Michelle Geltman at the Supernode Conference in 2023. "No? You've never heard of BD impact points? Well, that's because we made it up." Geltman is the senior director of business development at Branch, the company behind the industry's leading mobile linking and measurement platforms. She continued, "Before implementing ELG best practices, our partner team's biggest issue was that our metrics weren't aligning with Branch's overall metrics as a business. We were looking inward into how to measure our partnerships without taking into consideration what the business considers valuable."

Geltman and her team have come a long way since those early days. "The first step was to look inward and change our own mindset on how the partnership team is going to add value to the rest of the organization. How can we identify how to help the rest of the organization do their jobs better?"

To do this, Geltman studied the KPIs that were used to measure success inside every team of Branch's go-to-market organization: generating a sales pipeline, closing that pipeline, and retaining those customers over the long run. Branch's partner team shifted their goals to precisely match the outcomes and units of measurement used by their go-to-market counterparts.

This is how you should do it too. While the precise KPIs may vary from company to company, the one thing that partner teams consistently do when going through this exercise is move "closer to the bone" of revenue growth.

ELG efforts are go-to-market efforts, full stop. They are here to grow your company's revenue. The harder it is to connect the goals of your ELG efforts to the goals of your go-to-market team, the more you have lost your way.

This is one of those things that feels painfully obvious but still needs to be said out loud. Perhaps that's because generations of partnership leaders have been burned by the domino effect behind the partner paradox:

- Poor data availability leads to measurement issues.
- Measurement issues lead to measuring what you can.
- Measuring what you can tends to result in metrics that are dissociated from core business goals.
- Metrics that are dissociated from core business goals aren't taken seriously, even when the team is delivering outcomes that actually are improving go-to-market KPIs.
- When over-performance isn't believed, investment isn't made.

But ecosystem-led growth breaks this cycle. It is specifically tied to revenue-generating outcomes and powered by a new data layer that eliminates the blindness of the past that led to settling for weak KPIs.

If you adopt ELG, you must also measure your success using the same KPIs that your go-to-market teams and company are using. The only question then becomes how much of this attainment you can attribute back to your ELG efforts.

So let's talk about attribution.

Attributing Success to ELG

Attribution is the holy grail of partner professionals. If you remember the partner paradox from earlier in this book, there is a known gap between how partner teams feel they contribute to business growth and the credit they receive for that impact.

In ecosystem-led growth, we start to see an opportunity to do better. The interactions with partners and direct actions taken by them constitute an undeniable moment of influence, and often outright deal origination, that can be measured and reported upon.

Sourced Versus Influenced Outcomes

In cases where an entire revenue outcome would not have existed at all if not for the ELG effort, we use the term *sourced outcomes* (or *partner sourced outcomes* in many companies, as the specific action or insight from a specific partner tends to be at the core of the origination).

Sourced outcomes, specifically sourced revenue, are the gold standard and pack a serious punch as a KPI for your ELG efforts. For reasons listed earlier, however, many partner teams aren't able to be held accountable to this metric. This is because they don't have the data or playbooks in place to create and measure these kinds of outcomes. ELG is the answer here because its playbooks, which we explore in the next section, create measurable inflection points in the trajectory of the deal through which direct attribution is deserved and observable:

- Originating new leads that otherwise would not be accessible;
- Converting existing leads to qualified opportunities that otherwise would not have been converted;
- Converting opportunities into paying deals that otherwise would not have been won; and
- Expanding existing customers that otherwise would have remained at a flat revenue rate or churned.

Every playbook you are about to read is designed to create an outcome on the list above and create an evidence trail in the process.

Of course, there are also no shortage of instances in the earlier list where ELG moves the needle, but other factors may have played a role. What happens, for example, when a lead is generated through an ad campaign, but then an ELG tactic is what turns it into a qualified opportunity? How about when an SDR sources an opportunity, but an ELG tactic leads to your company winning that deal against a competitor?

Surely other parties will seek and deserve credit in these situations—and in many cases they may be the first or last touch on a deal, with ELG sitting somewhere in the middle. These circumstances are called **influenced** (or **partner influenced**) outcomes.

As we step into this realm, you may think, "Bob, take a dose of your own medicine! Partner influence is one of those made-up metrics you warn against that is just a little too squishy to be legitimate in the eyes of your go-to-market team." That's true with no data behind them but not with ELG.

Legacy partner metrics that are based on "influence" have a bit of a he-said-she-said problem baked into them. The influence in question is determined by a partner team's self-reported interaction or involvement in a deal, which sellers or other influencers don't always interpret or remember in the same way. The eyerolls ensue, the metrics are tossed aside, and the partnership team remains at the kids' table.

With ELG in place, influence takes on a whole new meaning. You now have a mountain of data that allows you to calculate, at a company-wide scale and with statistical significance, the difference between the deals where ELG influence is claimed and those where it is not.

This allows you to put your money where your mouth is. If ELG influence on opportunities isn't real, why do they close at a higher percentage rate? Why are deal cycles faster? Why are deal sizes larger? ELG lets you capture influence at scale and then show these facts outright.

Here's how.

Measuring Attribution

Once you have a framework in mind for measuring and reporting attribution, the trick is where and how to do it. ELG platforms such as Crossbeam can do this for you using a streamlined attribution model that pulls in data from your partner network, records of interactions between you and partners, and allows for manual tagging to tell the complete story of partner sourced and influenced revenue (see Figure 9.1).

FIGURE 9.1 Partner attribution tagging in Crossbeam.

Critically, that attribution history can then be automatically synced back to a CRM system such as Salesforce to allow it to live in the system of record where other points of influence are also tracked. In other words, ELG creates a source of truth for partner influence that works in the exact same way and lives in the exact same place as the other investments to which your company attributes revenue attainment.

Of course, ELG platforms aren't the only means of tracking influence. Some companies build partner influence and tracking directly into their CRMs using custom objects or fields.

There are also some amazing innovations emerging around attribution and influence tracking that allow for automated detection of potential partner influence. A forthcoming Crossbeam integration with Gong, for example, watches for any time a partner's name is mentioned on a sales call with an open opportunity. These mentions can be flagged as potential signals of influence so the attribution tagging doesn't get missed (or can even be applied automatically).

Regardless of whether you have a home-grown tracking solution or an elegant automated algorithm keeping the tally, what you end up with is very consequential: the ability to look at any given customer and say with confidence whether or not they were sourced or influenced by your partner ecosystem.

Once you have this dimension on your revenue data, you can start pulling some key figures that underscore the impact of ELG within your business:

- **Raw metrics:** The total customer count and revenue dollars sourced and influenced by your ELG motions;
- **Comparative metrics:** The relative improvement in deal speed, close rates, competitive win rates, **average contract values**, and retention rates for customers sourced or influenced by ELG as compared to those who weren't; and
- **Aggregate impact:** The aggregate lift in overall customer lifetime value when ELG strategies are in the mix on the acquisition and retention of that account.

You can also slice and dice each of these metrics down to any individual partner or group of partners to see the specific impact of a given relationship, sector, or strategy.

Here are just a few comparative insights featured on our blog in recent years, which are a result of doing these exact kinds of analyses:

- RingCentral upsells 3x as frequently with partners than without, and the dollar amount of those upsells is 4x the rate of upsells with no partners involved.
- Partner-influenced opportunities close 50% faster than any other deal at Freshworks.
- At Syncari, partner-influenced deals have conversion rates that are 2x higher and close faster than any non-partnership deal.
- Hatch boosts its close rate by 24% by incentivizing its partners' reps to co-sell.
- At Yotpo, 60% of overall referrals a month on average are influenced by partner marketing.
- Census sees 34% higher annual contract values (ACV) on partner-influenced deals.
- LeanData sees 24% higher annual contract values (ACV) on partner-influenced deals.
- At RollWorks, 80% of deals are partner-influenced, and those deals have 30% higher retention rates.
- Everflow Partner Marketing Platform sees 44% faster deal cycles when partners are involved.

Notice the KPIs at play here: revenue, deal size, close rates, time to close, churn prevention, and **expansion rates**. By choosing to measure success in these terms, the owners of the ELG strategy are speaking the language of go-to-market leadership, the CEO, and the board of directors.

Eliminating Partner Team Baggage

This section is another case where your "business book bingo card" is about to stay empty. You may expect guidance here on how to structure partnership teams, including titles, org charts, reporting structures, compensation, and more.

This, too, is tempting as a way to fill pages. After all, the partner account manager (PAM) title is so widely adopted that we named the Crossbeam mascot Pam (see Figure 9.2).

FIGURE 9.2 Pam and Bob at the Supernode 2023 Conference.

But here's the thing: If you're interested in benchmarks and data on these topics, you can check out the various State of the Partner Ecosystem reports published by Crossbeam since 2020. The data is there, among countless other places.

I've chosen not to include a discussion of these topics here because of what the data tells us: good leaders and managers will structure their teams in the way that makes sense given their goals, strengths, talent, and the nuances of their companies. Those structures will change over time as these factors evolve. We see big disparities in the way partner teams are structured across wildly successful companies of different industries and sizes, making the idea of a universal best practice in this area an unnecessary ideal.

I prefer to come at the discussion of ELG teams from a different angle. Remember, ecosystem-led growth is bigger than partnerships. When we talk about ELG team structure, that shouldn't look like a discussion on how to structure partnerships teams. It should look like a discussion on ELG ownership and expectations at the company level.

For ELG to work, partnerships must evolve from a siloed team to something that is infused in the various operations of a company. This is a prerequisite for the partner ecosystem getting credit, creating more sourced and influenced outcomes, and not needing to create an enormous team in order to generate an enormous impact.

Another outcome of this approach is that it achieves the important outcome of shedding the "baggage" of the old way of doing partnerships. Many senior executives have spent decades in organizations where partnerships ran the old way, before the existence of ELG data and playbooks. In those worlds, well-meaning partner professionals suffered from the challenges we've discussed, and the leaders around them failed to see proven value materialize.

We need to shake off this reputation, but old habits die hard and reputations can be hard to repair. Properly framing the role of the partnership team in ELG is critical.

> In ELG, partnership teams aren't babysitters or credit thieves. Their job is to create ecosystem ubiquity within their companies by becoming a force multiplier for the go-to-market team. They scale this value and the ecosystems they cultivate without scaling expenses.

In the upcoming playbooks section, you won't see motions that require hiring more humans or creating new titles in order to drive success. The ELG way is to infuse the leverage and intelligence that your partner ecosystem provides into the foundational ways that work gets done in the rest of your go-to-market organization.

Push Versus Pull

When ELG is successfully deployed, companies can see a radical shift from a "push" mentality to a "pull" mentality around how internal team members derive value from the partner ecosystem.

In the traditional "push" mentality, partnership teams would be responsible for identifying opportunities to get involved in accounts, inserting themselves into those pursuits, and earmarking their own influence on successful deals.

Sound familiar? This is how most partner teams work. In addition to being labor intensive and incremental in nature, any sales rep willing to be honest with you will admit that it can be annoying. Yes, the partner team's intent is to be value-additive, but they can also get it wrong. To a sales rep who is nurturing a fragile deal or knows context that can't be gleaned from the notes in the CRM, the wrong "push" at the wrong time can feel like an unwelcome annoyance at best.

In ELG, a "pull" mentality emerges. In this superior mode of operating, sellers, marketers, and customer success professionals have data and context derived from the partner ecosystem directly inside their systems of record. The presence and relevance of that data causes them to originate partner involvement themselves, either by pulling in a resource from the partnership team or self-servicing by directly using the data or even engaging with the partner company directly.

The end result is a step closer to ecosystem ubiquity. The data and relationships that stem from the partner ecosystem aren't a closely guarded and managed tool of a small team but instead a resource for the entire company that is simply cultivated by that team.

Unmanaged Partners

Another artifact of ELG is that partner professionals are able to meaningfully automate the assessment, onboarding, and management of their long-tail partners.

In the old way of doing partnerships, where data is rare and relationship capital is the currency of the job, every partner is a "managed partner." In other words, there is someone on your company's partnership team whose job is to invest time and energy into extracting value from that partnership. If team members were to stop conducting check-in calls, business reviews, and discovery sessions, then the partnership would languish in obscurity and rarely, if ever, generate value for your company.

In ELG, a new paradigm emerges. Using ecosystem data and ELG platforms, partner value is systemically derived on an ongoing basis from data sharing, automations, and the "pull" behaviors of go-to-market teams as described above. The playbooks in the remainder of this book lay out how this is done.

This model creates a long tail of "unmanaged partners" who do far more than languish on a list somewhere—they follow a narrow set of high-impact, low-maintenance ELG plays on an ongoing basis, with opportunities automatically surfacing and go-to-market teams self-servicing. The aggregate effect of this large pool of unmanaged partners can be very material.

When it comes to partnerships, there are unfortunately a lot of mixed experiences floating around out there. Introducing a new way of leveraging the partner ecosystem to drive growth requires doing the hard work of overcoming that history.

Avoid the temptation to put ELG on an island. Instead, earn that buy-in:

- Use the data the ELG platform provides to frame success in the metrics and language that the rest of your company understands.
- Enact playbooks that create undeniable quantitative proof of ROI and impact of ELG efforts.
- Grow away from the legacy strategy of "pushing" influence into deals, instead opting to use technology and training to establish a "pull" mentality among your go-to-market teams.
- Focus your partner team on achieving ecosystem ubiquity, and supercharge their internal ROI by focusing human time on only the highest-leverage partnerships while still deriving value from a huge long tail of unmanaged partners.

Only through these steps can the partner ecosystem and the people who manage it step away from the kids' table and become one of the most critical functions in your business.

10 Overcoming Security and Privacy Objections

Want to raise eyebrows? Try starting a company related to "data sharing" in the months after GDPR makes data privacy a top priority at every company. Try convincing public companies to entrust their proprietary sales data to a start-up. Try solving a cold-start problem so gnarly that no company has even bothered trying.

That was Crossbeam in 2018. As the world's first and most successful ELG platform, we've since earned the trust of over 15,000 companies, including hundreds of publicly traded enterprises. That journey has included countless security audits, risk assessments, questionnaires, and interviews.

Sitting here today, I can count on one hand the number of companies that chose not to move forward with Crossbeam—and thus the data and privacy foundations of ELG—for security or privacy reasons. If you're expecting questions in your organization about these areas, rest assured that the answers exist and are very strong.

This chapter is a critical path for inspiring confidence in ELG within both your company and your ecosystem. Even if your company has lower security and privacy standards than most, this still matters because your partners will need these answers too. This chapter can prepare you for any questions about how this all works and why.

When we zoom out, it's easy to see patterns in how companies evaluate the risk of adopting ELG and ELG platforms. In our experience, every question that arises fits into one of these two simple categories:

- "Can I trust my ELG platform?"
- "Does ELG itself expose me to risk?"

In order for ELG to work for your company, both of these questions need to be answered in a satisfactory manner. So let's get started.

Can I Trust My ELG Platform?

ELG platforms such as Crossbeam directly enable ecosystem-led growth practices by hosting a network of connected companies, facilitating controlled data sharing, and providing workflows for executing on ELG playbooks.

This question of "Can I trust my ELG platform?" pertains to the underlying security, policies, and overall trustworthiness of the ELG platform itself.

Note that this doesn't extend to the implications of partner data sharing or what happens to your data even when the platform works properly (which we cover next). Right now, we just want to figure out whether the ELG platform itself is a safe place for your company's data. Think of it as checking if a car's brakes work before worrying about the road trip's itinerary.

Here are some of the more specific questions you might encounter that fall into this category:

- Will we get approval to connect our CRM data to this platform?
- What happens if this platform has a data breach?
- Can you fill out and pass a security questionnaire?
- What external reports, audits, and certifications can the platform provide?

These questions are the same ones that get asked of every other SaaS tool or vendor that has access to your CRM data. Your company has likely evaluated (and approved) dozens if not hundreds of these tools, and the process for doing so is well documented and understood.

Scrutiny is likely to be at a high level due to the cross-departmental nature of the product, the data visibility it requires to function, and the downstream connection it has to other privacy and compliance questions. The key to passing this side of the evaluation is simply choosing an ELG platform that has invested appropriately in its security posture and knows how to demonstrate it.

Below are just a few of the most important areas where we make such investments at Crossbeam. This isn't meant as a plug for our product so much as a representative sample of how your ELG platform should come armed to every audit, questionnaire, and phone call on this subject. Regardless of how you plan to build your ecosystem data layer and power the playbooks that appear in the chapters ahead, it's critical that the foundational technology you use has investments in line with the ones that follow.

Data encryption: Crossbeam encrypts all data in transit and at rest. When you connect a data source, the information synced to Crossbeam is encrypted via the highest possible version of Transport Layer Security (TLS). Once the data is in the Crossbeam platform, it is encrypted in our database with AES256 encryption. The keys for the database encryption are securely stored in AWS Key Management Service (KMS). Access to AWS KMS is strictly controlled and monitored.

SOC 2 Type II compliance: Crossbeam maintains compliance with the AICPA's SOC for Service Organizations Trust Services Criteria, commonly known as SOC 2. This practice ensures that Crossbeam maintains a robust set of security controls, policies, and practices that are validated by regular external audits. These include policies related to systems access, physical security, privacy policies, disaster recovery plans, incident response plans, and regular meetings of a Security and Disaster Management Committee.

ISO 27001 Information Security Management System Certification: Crossbeam maintains the globally recognized information security certification, ISO 27001. This certificate was audited and issued by the top auditing firm A-LIGN.

ISO 27701 Privacy Information Management System Certification: Crossbeam maintains the globally recognized data privacy certification, ISO 27701. This certificate was audited and issued by the top auditing firm A-LIGN.

Penetration tests: An external security firm is engaged quarterly to conduct penetration tests of Crossbeam's systems. These tests include automated scans and manual testing by security experts seeking to uncover vulnerabilities.

Security features in the product: Crossbeam has been built with a security-first mindset, allowing us to incorporate a number of features and options into our product that can make your deployment of the platform in line with your security requirements (see Figure 10.1). These include things such as:

- **Audit logs:** Crossbeam's Audit Log feature provides detailed logs of your users' activity in the Crossbeam platform. This allows you to see the who, what, when, and how of changes and activity in your account.
- **Data source controls:** When connecting with CRM systems, data warehouses, CSV files, and Google Sheets, Crossbeam allows you to control the precise data synced down to the individual field level. This allows you to restrict Crossbeam's access down to only the exact data that is relevant to your use of our platform.
- **Single sign-on (SSO):** Customers can implement Security Assertion Markup Language (SAML) single sign-on (SSO) through Crossbeam's SSO provider. This allows a customer's team to log in to Crossbeam using their existing corporate credentials.
- **User roles:** Crossbeam offers role-based access controls (RBAC) to help companies manage user permissions. You can customize user roles to regulate data visibility, partnership management, and data sharing.

FIGURE 10.1 The data sync selection tool in Crossbeam.

In aggregate, this combination of documentation, external validation, and product maturity are enough to pass even the most complex security evaluation. This will allow your ELG platform to gain access to the data it needs to start unlocking value.

Of course, there is also a more complex question we also need to address in order to allow you to start connecting with partners, sharing data, and truly unlocking the value of ELG.

Does ELG Itself Expose Me to Risk?

Even if your ELG platform works precisely how it is intended, your company is still left with an important question: Do we want to allow data sharing with partners, and in doing so, would ELG itself expose us to risks?

In our experience, each company's policies around data sharing and collaboration with partners is unique: some share openly with their entire ecosystem, some share nothing and rely on partners sharing with them, some only share with close partners when special partner agreements are in place, some set up a unique set of sharing rules for each partner, and some share with all partners but limit what data points are shared.

The common thread is that your ELG platform must provide you with control and visibility over how data sharing is deployed in your go-to-market organization. You can properly frame the risk profile of an ELG strategy by building up three foundational layers:

1. **The purpose of ELG platforms:** Giving a clear definition of what an ELG platform is and the purpose and nature of data sharing in this context;
2. **ELG platform features that contain risk:** A clear description of the product features that ensure absolute control over your data and how it is used for ELG; and
3. **Common data-sharing strategies:** A library of strategies and techniques that allow your privacy and compliance teams to choose the data-sharing posture that is appropriate for their risk tolerance.

Ahead, we'll break down these three key areas.

The Purpose of ELG Platforms

Even before we wrote the first line of Crossbeam code, we drew lines in the sand around what Crossbeam and its network would and would not be. This explanation, shared below, has served us extremely well as an opening explainer in our privacy and legal assessments.

Crossbeam is an ELG platform. We directly enable ecosystem-led growth practices by hosting a network of connected companies, facilitating controlled data sharing between those companies, and providing workflows for executing on ELG playbooks.

Crossbeam's network is made up of company-to-company partnerships. The connective tissue of our network is made up of partnerships between our customers. These partnerships also exist independently of our platform, and we are simply a digital codification of a network graph that already exists in the real world.

Data sharing on Crossbeam is customized to meet the needs of each underlying partnership. Your company has ultimate control over the extent to which data may or may not be shared with each of its partners. Sharing is also one-directional, so there is no requirement to share reciprocally with partners. Crossbeam enables highly specialized rules for sharing specific slices of data under specific circumstances, such as overlaps in sales pipeline or customer sets.

Crossbeam is not a co-op. In a co-op, large numbers of companies who may or may not have relationships or connections to each other in the real world pool their data in order to create an aggregate data asset that gets returned to the group. On Crossbeam, any given company only has access to data from the specific partner companies that have opted into working with them and specifically granted them access to data.

Crossbeam is not a marketplace. In a marketplace, buyers and sellers gather to discover and exchange data assets for money. On Crossbeam, data is not bought or sold.

Crossbeam is not a data broker. Our business model is to earn subscription SaaS revenue by selling user seats and advanced features, not by selling our customers' data.

Crossbeam is focused on business data. The vast majority of use cases for Crossbeam and ELG can be accomplished through the sharing of data about companies, not people. The inclusion of **personally identifiable information (PII)** is optional and rare.

Crossbeam is a privacy enhancement. Whether you know it or not, individuals at your company are almost certainly engaged in traditional account-mapping practices. These involve spreadsheets of sensitive data being shared directly with partners through channels such as email on a regular basis. Crossbeam pulls this "shadow IT" practice into the daylight, reduces unwanted data leakage, and hands control and transparency over to the appropriate teams.

ELG Platform Features That Contain Risk

It is essential that your privacy, compliance, and legal teams understand how an ELG platform actually works and the mechanics by which partners are managed and data is made available to them.

The features detailed below show how Crossbeam specifically solves for these requirements by offering your company an immense amount of power to enforce data policies and contain risk.

Partnerships: Crossbeam partnerships are double opt-in. In order for a partnership to be established, a user with appropriate permissions from each party must explicitly approve the creation of the partnership. Even after this agreement, data remains protected until **data sharing rules** are enacted by the sharing party or parties.

Curated match lists: Instead of sharing raw data directly with partners, Crossbeam allows users to create **populations**, sometimes called "match lists." These are filtered lists, typically containing records such as "Active Opportunities" or "Customers," tailored-based on attributes from your CRM. Custom populations can be built to ensure a high degree of customization, and bespoke filtering is applied when appropriate.

Data-sharing rules: These rules determine which data partners can see. Only authorized users can set or change these rules, ensuring that data is shared according to specific criteria and under specific conditions for each partner or dataset.

You can picture each data-sharing rule as taking on the structure shown in Figure 10.2. The "match condition" in the structure determines which

```
if [match condition is met]:
    then share:
        [data to share]
    with:
        [partner]
```

FIGURE 10.2 Simple match-based sharing logic.

records (think "rows" in a spreadsheet) are to be shared with a partner. These match conditions can take on a few distinct forms:

- *Never share:* Crossbeam provides the option of hiding any given population from any partner, meaning no match condition will ever be met for that specific data.
- *Share overlapping records:* The most common match condition, this causes information to be shared only for the specific records in your population that also exist in the population of your partner. Only data from the overlapping records (that is, customers in common or overlapping sales pipeline) is included in the share.
- *Always share:* This is also known as "whitespace" or "greenfield" sharing and is used when you wish to share the entire contents of a population with your partner. Every record in that population will be included in that share.

Then, when applicable, the "data to share" setting determines which fields (think "columns" in a spreadsheet) are included in the shared records. It can take these forms:

- *Share overlap counts:* You can share just summary statistics about overlapping data without exposing any specific individual records.
- *Share specific fields:* You can select the exact fields within the shared records to expose to your partner. Some companies choose to share only their own business data (that is, which salesperson owns the account), while others may share more information about the nature of their relationship with the matching entity or more.

Transparency and reporting: Once your data sharing settings are configured, users with the appropriate permissions can review and monitor these rules and how they are applied via Crossbeam's user interface or audit logs.

Common Data Sharing Strategies

Now that the capabilities that allow your team to control risk are well understood, the only remaining question is how to use these features to enforce a certain data-sharing strategy that matches the risk posture of your company.

Following, we share several example strategies deployed within our ecosystem. They include approaches for configuring your data-sharing rules as well as tactics for controlling or decreasing the risk of your sharing approach. We often see these strategies used in combination with each other with different approaches being deployed based on the partner in question, the population being shared, or the goals of the collaboration. In Chapter 12, "The ELG Playbook Map," in the next part, we'll share some real-world examples of how companies such as Intercom use these strategies to manage sharing at scale within their ecosystems.

We want to reiterate that we are not your attorneys, and this document is in no way meant to be a replacement for a proper review of your strategy through the lens of your own company policies, agreements, and restrictions. This chapter is neither legal advice nor a contract and does not create any legal rights or obligations. This is simply meant as a set of illustrative examples to help frame out options for how to approach using Crossbeam.

Popular Sharing Strategy: Account Mapping

Account mapping is the most common sharing strategy employed by Crossbeam customers.

In this strategy, all data shares are triggered by "overlaps"—basically, data gets shared when a person or company in your population matches a person or company in your partner's population. Standard populations include prospects, opportunities, and customers.

Here, you are only revealing information to a partner when they also have some level of relationship with the matching person or company. All that is being conveyed is the context that you, too, have a certain level of relationship with them.

Companies will then typically share different fields from the matching records based on which populations match with the partner. For example:

- When your customers match the partner's target prospects, you may wish to protect your customer's data because the partner has less of a relationship with the customer or obligation to either the customer's company or to you. Perhaps only share the name of the account manager on your team who owns the customer account.
- When your customers match their customers, you may wish to share a larger amount of data or context as there is potentially a deeper

relationship between the partner and customer and therefore, less privacy expectations on both ends of the data-sharing relationship.

Conservative Sharing Strategy: Inbound Only

Since all data-sharing rules are one-directional, it is entirely possible to have an ecosystem of partners who are all sharing data with you but for you not to reciprocally share back.

While this may feel like it violates the Golden Rule, many companies, especially large ones who are at the center of their ecosystems, deploy an "inbound only" strategy by default. In this strategy, partners allow visibility into overlaps without the same being shared back.

The partners who are sharing data are motivated to do so because the other party will use that information to help them in some way. Another common example of this setup happens with referral partners. Those partners may be willing to share leads with a vendor, but the vendor needs to maintain secrecy around what is already in their CRM.

This setup could also be used by non-sharing partners who then use inbound data to initiate co-selling or co-marketing activities, make introductions, share information through other channels, or provide access to special promotions, partnership tiers, or collaborations.

Conservative Sharing Strategy: Summary Metrics Only

This is an extremely conservative approach in which no data about specific companies or people is shared whatsoever. Instead, all populations are set to share "overlap counts" only.

This strategy may be useful for identifying partners with the highest count of overlapping customers or prospects, but where the knowledge of who those accounts are is not required or able to be shared. There are many use cases for even this limited level of data.

Aggressive Sharing Strategy: Open Sharing

The most liberal use of an ELG platform involves sharing large amounts of data openly with all partners in all situations. In this scenario, default data-sharing rules are set up that allow visibility into all desired fields.

While this may seem aggressive, there are a number of scenarios where it has been deemed appropriate by our users. Some common situations include:

• Use cases involving close strategic partners where appropriate agreements are in place that protect the privacy and security of any shared data;

- Use cases where the data being shared is public or otherwise non-proprietary, but Crossbeam is useful for tracking overlaps, creating overlap-driven workflows, and managing collaboration between multiple parties; and
- Internal use cases where Crossbeam is used to collaborate between disparate sales teams, as part of a post-acquisition integration process or across various subsidiaries.

Strategy Enhancement: Excluding Personally Identifiable Information (PII)

An ELG platform's granular controls should make it easy to exclude personal information from the platform at any level. As described earlier, this can be done initially upon data sync (excluding personal information from the platform entirely), at the time of population creation (excluding personal information from potential sharing rules), or in the data-sharing rules themselves (blocking personal information from reaching specific partners).

Here are a few examples of how you can enact PII-sharing restrictions:

- Only **company-level information** is shared, such as business name, funnel stage, or firmographic data. No information is shared about the contacts you have at any company.
- Some **contact-level information** is shared, but any personal information is scrubbed. The most common example here would be sharing the title of your contacts but not their names or contact information.
- **Personal information** is only revealed when the partner already has this same exact matching personal information inside their own data. If you have a population made up of people, matches are based on email addresses. While email addresses are personal information, they will only match in cases where the partner already knows that email address. This ensures that you are not divulging any personal information that the partner had their own independent ownership of before the data share.

Note that many companies using ELG platforms will share the personal information of their own employees (such as the work email address of the account executive who owns an account). Information about your own employees is a different class of personal information that is treated differently from customer data.

Strategy Enhancement: Creating Broad Populations to Hide Relationship Types

One piece of metadata that gets revealed by overlap comparisons is which population(s) a matching company is part of. For example, even if you are only sharing the names of overlapping companies, the fact that a matching company was in your "Customers" population reveals the nature of your relationship with them as well.

In cases where you don't want to reveal any implied data, such as the funnel stage or customer status of an overlapping account, you can opt to keep your populations broad and nonspecific.

For example, you may deploy this strategy by creating one big population: "All Named Accounts." This population contains every company where you have a relationship but doesn't specify who is a customer, who is a prospect, and so on. If there is a match, you can then opt to share more data based on the partner and circumstances, but you haven't indirectly revealed any information through the way your populations are segmented.

Strategy Enhancement: Excluding Specific Companies or People

In some cases, you may wish to exclude a specific list of companies from the ELG platform entirely. This may be highly guarded accounts or ones where special privacy terms exist.

Your platform should make it easy to exclude individual companies or people from the data-sharing process. There could be a few approaches depending on your needs:

- Your population builder should provide an extremely flexible user interface (UI) for filtering what data appears in any given population. Individual companies or people can be specified within the population definition itself to ensure they are hard-excluded from the results in all circumstances.
- If there is a custom property in your CRM data that indicates which customers to exclude (a "custom NDA" checkbox, for example), you can use the population builder to exclude all records with that property across the board.
- If you only wish to exclude certain accounts for specific partners, you can create custom restricted populations just for those partners

and "hide" your normal populations from them. This will provide them with a typical experience for that partner but with the excluded accounts removed.

Strategy Enhancement: Customizing Legal Language

In addition to the strategies deployed within your ELG platform, you may also wish to augment your partnership agreements, privacy policies/data processing or data protection provisions, nondisclosure agreements, or even the communication you have surrounding Crossbeam usage. Check with your legal team for help with these concepts. Here are a few examples:

- Partnership agreements typically contain provisions binding the partner to certain confidentiality and privacy requirements as it relates to data shared in executing the partnership. Some companies review or update their agreements to ensure either that such provisions exist and allow the flexibility to use the ELG platform or that partnership agreements are executed between their company and those they partner with on the platform.
- When sending an invitation to partner with another company through the platform, companies should be allowed to use a custom invite link feature rather than an in-product invite. This allows them to send the invite link in an email or other official communication along with language reaffirming that data collaboration is governed by partnership agreements, NDAs, and/or other governing documents.
- The data governed by your privacy policy may or may not be the kind of data you are sharing in the platform (i.e. personal information may or may not be shared in your use case). In the event that such information is shared, some clients review or modify their privacy policy to ensure that sharing this data with third parties is appropriately disclosed and permitted.

There's more than one way to make a data-driven partnership. While most companies choose a simple data-sharing strategy that works well for them, any ELG platform worth its weight should make it possible to do much, much more. Your ELG platform should allow your company to deploy as nuanced and controlled a data-sharing strategy as you require. From the broadest default settings to curating an individual data point, you can develop a strategy that works for you and your company's needs.

We spoke earlier about the pre-ELG world where fragments of these strategies were pieced together through phone calls and spreadsheets being emailed between companies. Those practices are fundamentally broken from a risk management standpoint and inherently unscalable due to the issues they create in this area.

What ELG offers is a holistic solution to this problem. It brings data collaboration across companies into the light, takes on the privacy and security requirements of each business through transparent and well-documented controls, and allows ELG to be a technique that scales legitimately and proudly at the forefront of your company, rather than under the radar and relegated to bite-size fragments of value.

Powering Up Your Account Mapping Matrix

Remember those spreadsheets we mentioned in the previous part that used to get emailed around between just about every partner team on the planet? Those were in service of a practice known as **account mapping**—or, simply put, trying to figure out how your company's accounts overlap with a partner's.

In the old days, account mapping worked something like this:

- Decide which account lists you'd like to compare with your partner.
- Build reports in your CRM to isolate them.
- Hand-curate your list down to ones you think might overlap with your partner without exposing too much data.
- Decide which account-level data you'd like to share with your partner. For example: name, company, and some kind of sales rep contact info is typically the minimum.
- Export the data as a CSV.
- Ask your partner to do the same. If possible, structure your data using the same fields and same column order.
- Load or import the data into a cloud or file-sharing service. Some partnership managers have told us they use several Google Sheets tabs. (And we've seen them; it gets unwieldy.)
- Search for matches. You can use VLOOKUP, but many partnership managers end up comparing both sheets manually.

The downsides to account mapping with spreadsheets are many:

- **It's inaccurate.** Without standardization across your account lists and your partner's, there's an insurmountable amount of room for error. For example: Your partner refers to Adobe Marketo as "Marketo" in their CRM, and your company has all Adobe subsidiaries under the name "Adobe." Oh and what if you're selling to Delta Faucets, and your partner is selling to Delta Airlines? There's an infinite number of variations you and your partner could have for various accounts, from nomenclature, to subsidiaries, to company websites. Cue: the Google Sheet headache.
- **It's time consuming.** Consider all of the false negatives you'd have to navigate through (like Marketo not matching up with Adobe) plus the need to continuously map accounts with each partner regularly. There's no automation, so if you map accounts on a Thursday, you could easily miss a huge opportunity on Friday. Make sure to set big chunks of time aside on your calendar each week to keep your partner data up to date—well, almost.
- **It's not secure.** In order to map accounts the old way, one side has to give up its data first. NDA or not, most companies are extremely uncomfortable sharing full account lists or sales pipelines. In the era of GDPR and CCPA this can make account mapping a non-starter. This is a weak Band-Aid on the prisoner's dilemma issues we mentioned earlier, and risk is poorly managed in doing so.
- **It's instantly out of date.** The moment the spreadsheet is exported, it's frozen in time. You can only get up-to-date data on your partnerships by starting over.

When there are five, ten, or twenty partners, each step can get exponentially more time consuming as the data complexity and dimensionality of your self-managed, spreadsheet-based dataset grows (see Figure 11.1).

Ecosystem-led growth starts with reimagining the process of account mapping to take partner teams from the archaic and flawed spreadsheet-sharing methods to a more secure, managed, scalable process for surfacing overlaps and taking action on the results.

The best way to think of this opportunity space is as a simple three-by-three **account mapping matrix** (see Figure 11.2). In the matrix, the rows are your basic account segments (customers, opportunities, and prospects),

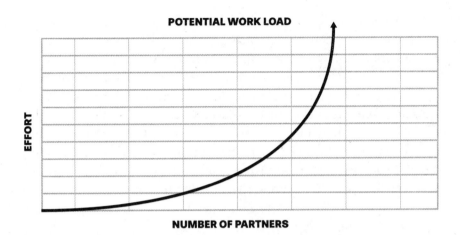

FIGURE 11.1 The exponential complexity of manual account mapping.

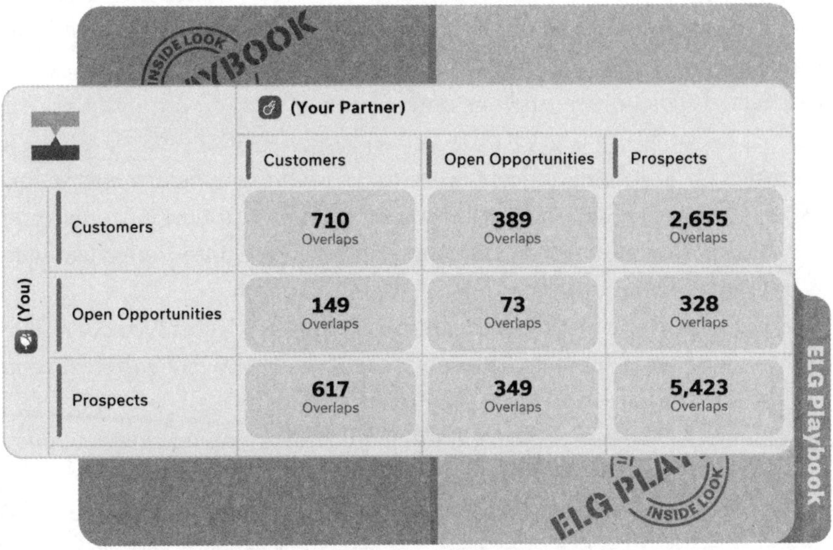

FIGURE 11.2 The account mapping matrix.

and the columns are a partner's same three basic account segments. Within each resulting cell is a universe of potential—it's the overlap between your data and that of your partner, resulting in nine distinct intersections of data that each can carry a way for you to exchange and create value together.

A core building block of any ELG playbook involves the data in the account mapping matrix. At Crossbeam, this is represented through the interface for each of your partners, from which you can click into any cell to see the full list of overlaps (assuming your partner has shared that data).

Zooming out from the data itself, you can envision this matrix as something more profound: it's a map of the many ELG playbooks that exist at the intersection of you and the partners in your ecosystem, with each square representing a play that sits somewhere in your revenue funnel, from the earliest stages of lead generation to the customer success playbooks around retention and expansion. In the chapters that follow, we'll walk through these playbooks in detail and highlight the squares of overlapping data that you'll use to power each of them.

While ecosystem-led growth can involve companies collaborating around data from any source of any type, the honest answer is that over 90% of Crossbeam users are building playbooks around three standard segments.

An account segment, also called a "population" or "match list," is simply a list of companies or people. Our standard segments are the three basic funnel stages that nearly every business can map their existing data onto: prospects, opportunities, and customers:

> **Prospects:** Any company or person that I wish my company was selling to. This is our list of target customers who fit our ideal customer profile but who are not yet customers and who are not yet engaged with us as potential buyers.
>
> **Opportunities:** These are the companies that are actively in our sales pipeline. They are being actively tracked and managed to drive toward a potential sale in a reasonable time frame.
>
> **Customers:** These are companies that are already paying clients of ours.

Now, as you can imagine, each of these segments has countless subsets and ways to slice and dice the data. There are also other valuable segments worth defining (churned customers is a popular example). But for the purposes of getting off the ground, we always start our users out with these three standard ones.

Every playbook and case study that follows in this section can be traced back to these data intersections. These ELG plays all use data as a foundational building block for success and scale. In the following chapters, we walk through the many methods and techniques used by leading companies to create, sustain, and measure value using ecosystem-led growth.

PART
4

The ELG Playbooks

12

The ELG
Playbook Map

Let's review: ecosystem-led growth is a go-to-market motion that focuses on the partner ecosystem as the primary way to attract, convert, and grow customer relationships.

Those three components—attracting, converting, and growing customers—are each complex motions on their own, often governed by different teams and interests inside of any given company. They ultimately make up your whole revenue funnel, reflecting the distinct jobs done by your marketing, sales, and customer success teams (see Figure 12.1).

Of course, there's more to ELG than simply being a force multiplier for your existing funnel. There is also a powerful value loop that comes into play.

As your ecosystem-led growth strategy comes to life, the success of driving more business through your partner ecosystem actually drives development of the ecosystem itself. More pipeline and customers means more data, more serviceable obtainable market, and more social proof—the raw ingredients for a thriving partner ecosystem. That ecosystem then becomes both an input and an output to your growth and the potential of your company.

Overlaying the important work of ecosystem development onto your go-to-market funnel yields a treasure map of sorts for us to follow. In the coming chapters, we'll dig for gold in the practice areas of ecosystem development (partnerships), pipeline generation (marketing), revenue generation (sales), and expansion (customer success) (see Figure 12.2).

FIGURE 12.1 The classic revenue funnel.

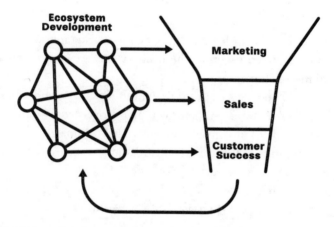

FIGURE 12.2 The ELG playbook map.

At this point, one thing is abundantly clear: ecosystem-led growth is not the work of the partnership team alone. Teams that manage and grow partner ecosystems are a necessary, but not sufficient, ingredient for the success of an ELG strategy. Equally important are the front-of-house teams to communicate directly with customers, sell them products, and grow their accounts.

The chapters that follow are therefore broken out not just by playbook but by persona. True students of ELG should read them all, as should CEOs and senior executives. Practitioners in partnerships, marketing, sales, and customer success can feel free to jump across each discipline to find the playbooks that matter most in their roles.

Regardless of your role, I hope the pages that follow become the most earmarked, referenced, and highlighted ones in this book. Let's begin our walk through the playbooks that will bring your company's ecosystem-led growth strategy to life.

13 Ecosystem Development: Populate Your Partner Ecosystem with Winners

Our first stop on the ELG playbook map is perhaps the most important of them all: ecosystem development. It is through ecosystem development strategies that companies identify the highest-value potential partners, build those relationships, and bring those partnerships to life (see Figure 13.1).

This is hardly a one-and-done motion. At every stage of your company's growth, these strategies are worth revisiting and your ecosystem is worth re-evaluating. Your company's North Star goals may evolve, as may the North Star goals around which you build your ecosystem.

Whether you're new to ecosystem building or a multi-decade veteran at a global enterprise, I can promise you one thing: finding potential partners won't be your biggest problem.

The explosion of the API economy, the enduring criticality of service providers, and the bundling-unbundling cycle of technology products are just a few factors that create a potential partner generation firehose. This might seem like good news on the surface, but unfortunately it turns out to be a problem in itself. In a world where potential partners are everywhere, a litany of trade-offs follow suit.

Partnerships, even "free" ones, aren't free. In the realm of tech partnerships, for example, the decision to build your own integrations or even support externally built integrations comes with engineering overhead, API development, maintenance implications, documentation, new customer success and training playbooks, and brand considerations. In the world

The ELG Playbook Map

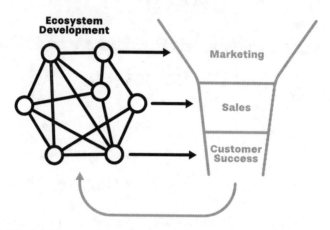

FIGURE 13.1   The ELG playbook map: ecosystem development.

of service partners, the overhead of training, incentives, and relationship management can be overwhelming.

When these partnerships pay off, the ROI is astronomically high, and these up-front costs feel nominal. But it's a journey. The return of value in any partner relationship follows a classic **J-curve** shape, as shown in Figure 13.2.

As shown in the figure, the up-front investment in new partnerships creates negative relationship value until returns gradually pull you out of the hole and break past the x-axis into positive-ROI territory. But getting to that point takes time, capital, and risk tolerance.

ELG's role in all this is to fix the J-curve problem by telling you which partners will have the fastest, sharpest climb to value and reach the highest peaks. No one can eliminate the J-curve entirely, but with this set of playbooks you can:

- Decrease the time period during which your J-curve is in that declining state during your early relationship;
- Increase how steeply the J-curve bends back up once new partnerships in your ecosystem come online;
- Pick smarter bets so that bad bets don't pull your average J-curve into less desirable shape overall; and

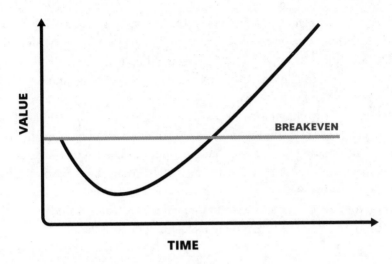

FIGURE 13.2 Classic J-curve shape.

- Uncap the ceiling on ecosystem value so that the upside of the curve continues to grow into perpetuity and each new cohort of partners in your ecosystem becomes a never-ending growth machine, just as we showed in the Crossbeam cohort analysis data earlier on.

A critical building block of such a modern ELG strategy is using ecosystem data to pick the right partners and allocate your time appropriately among them. This isn't about saving time just for your partner team; it ripples through to your sellers, support teams, and product builders as well. It refines and focuses your company's human time to just the highest-leverage areas representing the greatest potential for growth.

This practice disrupts the legacy motion of relying on personal relationship capital, flawed anecdotal data, or sunk cost fallacies to prioritize time investments in your partner ecosystem. You'll notice this as a recurring theme in the case studies in this section.

Prioritizing Partners

When it comes to picking winners, Gong sets the standard. We mentioned Gong a few chapters ago when talking about the race for dominance in the rapidly consolidating sales intelligence space. Gong has done an amazing job of growing from an upstart innovator in conversation intelligence to a force of nature in the fast-growing revenue intelligence category. More than 4,000 companies around the world rely on Gong to support their strategic initiatives, deal execution, forecasting, advanced coaching, and productivity to grow revenue efficiently.

Gong is a true champion of ecosystem-led growth, having built a flourishing partner ecosystem that powers a virtuous cycle of high-quality partners, value-creating integrations, and compounding customer impact.

At the helm of this rich ecosystem is Ashi Aber, the head of Technology Partnerships. Aber faces a high-class problem in his role: a constant firehose of new companies wish to integrate with Gong, pull data from its platform, or otherwise incorporate its technology into theirs.

"We get a flurry of new requests every day to build against our APIs," Aber told me in a recent conversation. "These come from a wide range of company types and sizes, including small start-ups working on skunkworks projects. But we also care deeply about fostering innovation in our ecosystem and don't want to miss any diamonds in the rough."

This is where Aber and his team are able to use modern account-mapping practices and ecosystem-led growth data to make sure they focus the right amount of energy on the right partners at the right time.

Out of protocol, new Gong partners sign an NDA that envisions using a modern account-mapping platform such as Crossbeam. From there, standard partner onboarding includes a baseline analysis of how much their current and target customer bases overlap, effectively providing a way to measure the **total addressable market (TAM)** of a given potential or existing tech integration.

This is a massive evolution in the process for evaluating potential partners. Remember the old ways of building partnerships when brand size, personal relationships, and chance encounters ruled the day? This is the exact opposite—hard data is table stakes, and those other factors simply add texture.

Imagine that you're in Aber's seat and evaluating three potential partnerships:

- Partner A is a huge public company with a big brand.
- Partner B is a small start-up that has networked their way to relationships with your C-suite.
- Partner C is an under-the-radar private company.

Your team is lean, and you really only have the time and resources to invest in one new integration this quarter. What do you do?

In the old days, this would have been quite the conundrum. Presumably huge partner A has the biggest addressable market, right? Sounds like a safe bet. But working with partner B might be lower friction in terms of internal politics and executive sponsorship. And partner C . . . well, intuition says we should probably put them on the backburner for now.

Now, imagine you've got the data on the TAM of each relationship (see Figures 13.3, 13.4, and 13.5).

A closer look at partner A reveals that, while they indeed have a massive customer base, the actual intersection with your ideal customer profile is, well, less than ideal. Their company TAM may be huge, but the TAM

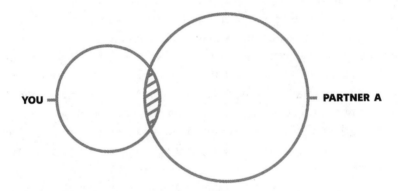

FIGURE 13.3 Big partner, small overlap.

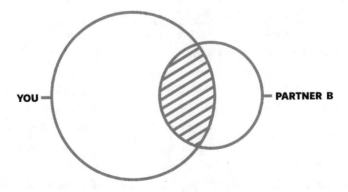

FIGURE 13.4 Small partner, modest overlap.

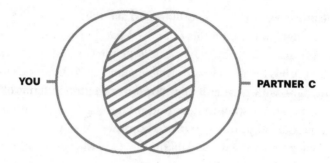

FIGURE 13.5   Peer-sized company with amazing overlap.

of your partnership is actually not as significant as some other players' because only a miniscule fraction of their customer base and target market overlaps with yours.

Partner B is a bit more interesting, as their small size has yielded a pretty small TAM right now but shows that a much, much higher percentage of their customer base overlaps with yours. This points to a high amount of alignment in your TAM and a relationship worth cultivating, although not something you'd likely count on to move the needle among a large portion of your existing customers at the moment. This might be a great case for asking them to do the legwork of building an integration or pursuing some co-marketing efforts to help build a joint pipeline first (more on that later).

Finally, let's look at the data behind that under-the-radar partner C.

Now what do we have here? As it turns out, partner C is the little engine that could. While more modest in size than partner A and potentially less flashy than partner B, it turns out that your ideal customer profile has very material overlap and the addressable market for an integration between your products would be applicable to a significant percentage of your existing customer base. We have a winner!

This is the kind of analysis you can take to the bank—it will outweigh relationship capital, brand cache, and circumstance to give you the right decision every time. These high overlaps in customers and sales pipeline between you and your key partners end up being one of the most important inputs to just about every strategy that gets laid out in playbooks ahead.

Why? These overlaps are the currency of value creation, and that value leads to more sales. "Customers who are leveraging integrations get more value from our platform, which translates to more business," Aber said.

"Those who use at least one of our downstream integrations have a healthy double-digit higher ACV on average."

Having the partner overlap data is critical not just in picking partners initially but in continuously investing in those partnerships over time. Because Gong knows how many overlapping customers they have with a given tech partner, they can measure adoption of integrations by percentage of TAM rather than more simplistic absolute counts.

According to Aber, "For example, if we see that across our highest-potential integrations the usage/adoption averages about 50% of the TAM, but one of them is only at 15%, that tells us something may be wrong from a value or product integration perspective. Then the product team can go in and start dissecting and analyzing what's going on here to make things right."

And thus we see the first mark of ELG impact, all the way at the top of your partner funnel. From the moment of partner selection, these data-driven decisions start having ripple effects on how much your partner ecosystem will ultimately move the needle for your business.

Curating Data Access

For Catherine Brodigan, senior manager of Global Partnerships at Intercom, ecosystem development goes beyond just picking partners. Her strategy also includes a framework for curating partner access to data and making sure that partners get the data they need only when it's appropriate to the breadth and depth of their partnership.

Intercom is a customer service platform built for an AI-first world. It sends over 600 million messages per month and enables interactions with over 800 million monthly active end users. Intercom categorizes partners into tiers and applies a "partner prioritization framework" powered by second-party ELG data from Crossbeam.

The Intercom team uses a combination of integration usage data and account-mapping data to classify partners into three tiers:

1. **The Partner Tier**
   (a) Entry requirements: The partner has built an Intercom app (integration) and is listed in Intercom's app store.
   (b) Focused on programmatic and scalable benefits, such as newsletter features, blog posts, and light co-marketing activities.

2. **The Plus Tier**
   (a) Entry requirements: same requirements as the Partner Tier, plus the partner has 100+ app installations.
   (b) Focused on identifying addressable audiences, target buyer personas, market segments, and territories for more tactical co-marketing activities. Sometimes these partners will send referrals to Intercom.
3. **The Premier Tier**
   (a) Entry requirements: invite only.
   (b) Focused on identifying GTM readiness for co-selling and determining overlaps with Intercom's ideal customer profile (ICP) using Crossbeam.

These tiers make it easier for Intercom to determine which partners they should map accounts with and how they should go to market with them.

The map of partner types allows Intercom to fairly and consistently stratify the level of collaboration and data access they provide to different partners. As partnerships grow and prove to be more valuable, so too do the number of go-to-market plays that get unlocked. For example, when account mapping, the Intercom team sticks to sharing only overlap counts (the number of overlaps in the account mapping matrix) with their "Plus" partners.

For "Premier" partners, the Intercom team runs more detailed account-mapping reports (sharing specific **data fields**). Brodigan's team is mostly focused on "Premier" partners, as this level of immersion offers the highest leveraged use of time for human collaboration. "We are going deeper with these Premier partners on account mapping and referrals, co-selling initiatives, territory-specific enablement, and more heavy co-marketing like joint webinars and events," she says.

Brodigan and her team use a "partner prioritization framework" to quantitatively and qualitatively evaluate which "Plus" and "Premier" partners they should double-down on.

Quantitative measures include:

- Number of mutual customers; and
- Total number of installs.

Qualitative measures include:

- ICP alignment;
- Partner engagement;
- Partner sales resources;
- Partner marketing resources;
- Account-mapping status;
- Partner brand presence;
- Historical partner marketing investments and results; and
- Future partner marketing potential.

"This framework is typically the entry point for account-mapping data for our team as it helps us size existing and potential future opportunities with our app partners," says Brodigan. This is how Intercom is able to move so quickly and strategically—they spend time with the highest-value partners.

The Partner Prioritization Matrix

In combination, the playbooks we've just seen from Gong and Intercom start to suggest a framework for holistically managing, measuring, and making decisions about investments in your partner ecosystem.

Enter Chris Lavoie, PhD. Chris has helped build out partner programs from within hypergrowth companies and as a consultant. These days, he is the founder of Ecosystem University, a Partnership Leaders Initiative. He knows a thing or two about spending the right time with the right partners. Chris has a novel approach to partner prioritization that combines the strategies we have already discussed into a living, breathing visualization of your partner ecosystem's health and opportunity.

His premise is that you can ultimately measure the potential of any given partnership by combining two critical data points:

- The **serviceable obtainable market (SOM)** of that partnership. This is more precise and useful than a TAM measurement (that is, your partner's whole market) or a similarly overstated addressable market based on your ideal customer profile. Instead, it uses ELG data from

Crossbeam to inform a universe of known, serviceable shared relationships based on real data that can be acted upon.

* The **value created for shared customers.** This is measurable as well—it's fair to presume that your value delivery is correlated well with customer health metrics such as speed to close, contract value, retention rates, and net promoter score (NPS). As such, it's possible to quantify the "lift" that shared customers with this partner experience relative to the rest of your customer list. Whatever your North Star metric or metrics, you can use ELG data to compare the customers you share with this partner to those you don't and map them against other partners in your ecosystem.

If you haven't figured it out by now, my love language is 2 × 2 matrices. Lavoie recommends that companies map out their current and prospective customers using the 2 × 2 matrix shown in Figure 13.6.

Plot each partner of yours as a dot on this matrix, and you'll end up with a rich scatterplot through which you can better understand your ecosystem, relatively prioritize partners, and establish a next best action for each one. Not only does this matrix provide you a means to visually understand four distinct quadrants of partner quality, but it also helps you use those quadrants to potentially inform next steps.

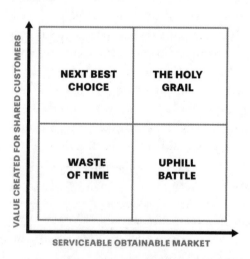

FIGURE 13.6 Lavoie's partner prioritization matrix.

Using Intercom's playbook from the previous section, we could easily map Lavoie's four quadrants to four ways of triaging your partner relationships:

- **The holy grail:** Choice priority partners deserving of human attention, technical investments, and regular business reviews.
- **Next best choice:** High-potential partners who may prove strategic in key deals but may not be a wellspring of new leads; they may invest resources, but don't rely on them for market development and demand generation at scale.
- **Uphill battle:** Huge overlapping market, but your joint value story leaves something to be desired; potentially great for co-marketing or reaching large audiences of overlapping ICP but not the "closer" you bring in to win or save a late-stage account.
- **Waste of time:** Watch and wait, but don't invest today. Don't toss these all to the curb—stay connected and revisit the data on SOM and fit over time. Very often a company can evolve its way from this quadrant into others quickly through a pivot or product-market-fit breakthrough.

The best thing about this matrix is that it's not static. Over time, as your own data and the data of your partners evolves, so too will their relative positions on this grid. By continuously reevaluating your most promising and investable partners, you can ensure that you're skating where the puck is going when it comes to ecosystem potential.

At the end of the day, this first stop on the ELG playbook map is more than just a stop—it's a journey. The infinite loop of ecosystem wins bolstering ecosystem demand and calling for more curation, more partnerships, and more outputs is a high-class problem that every company of scale will have to navigate.

Of course, this journey does not mean more people and more cost. The thoughtful, data-driven management of partner relationships and the long tail of partner opportunities is something that modern automated account mapping was made for. It constitutes a critical piece of the ELG machine that will keep your growth engine humming even as your company transitions through its own stages of growth and evolution.

14

Ecosystem-Led Marketing: Fill Your Funnel with Ecosystem Qualified Leads

With high-potential partners in place and the skeletal system of ecosystem-led growth wired up via automated account mapping, it's time to start our journey through your revenue funnel. We'll walk through each stage of your funnel, revealing the playbooks that make modern ELG companies thrive.

We begin with the practice of using ecosystem-led growth to drive a steady flow of qualified, efficient pipeline to the top of your revenue funnel. This is **ecosystem-led marketing**.

"The modern marketing playbook is an ecosystem-led playbook," says marketing pioneer Alina Vandenberghe, cofounder and co-CEO at Chili Piper. She would know—her company builds technology that helps thousands of modern revenue teams collect, distribute, and convert inbound leads.

According to Vandenberghe, "Nearly every best practice in demand gen, advertising, inbound, ABM, personalization, and automation can be leveled-up by infusing data, context, and relationships from your partner ecosystem. We've brought that mantra to life at Chili Piper, and it's had a powerful effect at every stage of our funnel."

Vandenberghe isn't alone. In this chapter, we'll navigate to the next piece of the ELG playbook map: the top of your revenue funnel (see Figure 14.1).

The ELG Playbook Map

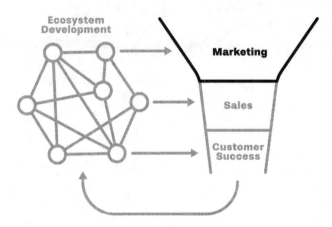

FIGURE 14.1 The ELG playbooks: ecosystem-led marketing.

The Ecosystem Qualified Lead (EQL)

A **lead** is the most primordial early indicator of revenue that exists in your funnel. It's not yet a real conversation, a qualified discussion, or something you can confidently project as future revenue. But it's a signal—a reason to believe that a particular person or company has the potential to become your customer at some point in the future. It's the first domino of growth, and ecosystem-led growth is exceptionally good at delivering leads.

We think of leads that are sourced through ELG tactics as **ecosystem-qualified leads**, or **EQLs** (pronounced "equals" by the nerdiest among us). An EQL is a lead that is more likely to become a paying customer due to behaviors it is exhibiting in your partner ecosystem.

Any good marketer can tell you that the origin story of a lead is a key input to its real value. In **product-led growth (PLG)** companies, for example, a **product-qualified lead (PQL)** is a lead that has exhibited behaviors in your product that indicate a propensity to buy. PQLs often prove to be higher-converting or more likely to engage than a lead that came in through a paid advertisement or a cold call.

So too is the logic behind EQLs. What makes them exist is a combination of intent and behavior. What makes them unique is that you are the only person on the planet who can piece together these exact behaviors, as the data is sourced by combining the aggregate knowledge from your partner ecosystem.

If you picture your long tail of ideal customers as a giant haystack, the knowledge from your partner ecosystem equates to the world's most powerful magnet. Run the magnet along your various target segments, user personas, and tech stacks, and watch as the needles in the haystack surface themselves by showing relationships, product adoption, and other behaviors that inform their likelihood to take interest in your product. From there, you can scale up various plays—which we'll explore in this chapter—for moving those EQLs into your buying process.

Peter Cummings is the head of the EMEA Stripe Partner Ecosystem. He's a veteran of fine-tuned revenue organizations including Adobe and Experian. And he's all in on EQLs. "The ecosystem-qualified lead is the key," Cummings told me on a recent visit to London. "In the old days, most partner meetings were more like therapy sessions. Why don't we get the credit we deserve? Why can't our impact be front and center in how the business reports on its performance? Well, in the new world of ELG, we can put partner teams on equal footing and qualify leads using data from our ecosystem."

As we learned earlier, an EQL is a lead that is more likely to become a paying customer due to behaviors it is exhibiting in your partner ecosystem. Those behaviors may include things such as purchasing or evaluating complementary tools, working with service partners in your space, or actively being pursued by partner companies who focus on your same customer profile. All of these are observable and collectable at scale via ELG platforms such as Crossbeam.

To Cummings, the EQL is something the marketing team can have some real ownership of (they love a good QL). It doesn't belong on a separate slide or sitting off on an island in the company's reporting. Quite the contrary, it's a new column on the most important reports in your business. The EQL is a first-class qualification metric that can live alongside marketing-qualified leads (MQLs), product-qualified leads (PQLs), and any other bespoke qualification metrics a company might have.

Most important, we finally have the data we need to prove that EQLs are, far and away, better leads. Here are some easy ways to prove it:

- Compare the rate at which EQLs convert to qualified opportunities when compared to other sources of leads.

- Compare the rate at which those opportunities convert to closed-won deals, the average contract values of those deals, the speed to close, and the long-term retention rate of those customers.
- Split this further into EQL by partner to get a sense of how different partners influence the ultimate value of a qualified lead—this is similar to the work done to qualify partners in Lavoie's 2 × 2 matrix from Chapter 13.
- Go retroactive. Even if you haven't been historically tracking EQLs, you can use ELG data from a platform such as Crossbeam to go back in time and see which of your opportunities from the past quarter or year were ecosystem-qualified at the time they were generated. How did these perform on these metrics against the rest of the pack? Even a manual analysis in a spreadsheet is enough fodder to prove an incredibly powerful point about tracking and leveraging EQLs as a core qualification metric for your company.

Now that we know what an EQL is and why it's so valuable, let's get to work creating them.

Generating EQLs with Second-Party Data

The only thing better than one lead is a whole list of them. The generation and qualification of lead lists is a core function of demand generation, and ELG offers new and powerful ways to enlist your partner ecosystem in that process. Such leads are inherently ecosystem-qualified, making these playbooks a goldmine of scalable lead generation for any marketing team.

"By tapping into a larger pool of relevant accounts through our overlapping partner data, utilizing dynamic lists, and serving specific relatable messaging via RollWorks ads, we've seen up to 60% higher engagement rates compared to using static data, leading to greater opportunities for revenue growth," says Jodi Cerretani, vice president of marketing at RollWorks.

Remember the account mapping matrix? The strategies employed here are the ones that sit in the bottom row: where your prospects overlap with the prospects, opportunities, and customers of your partners (see Figure 14.2). Using your partner ecosystem to bring these prospects to life is the secret sauce of ELG for marketers.

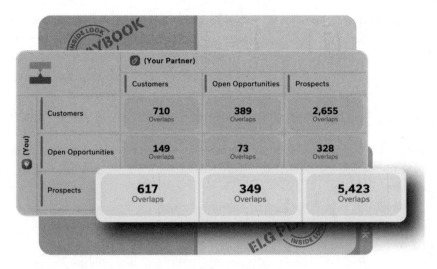

FIGURE 14.2 EQLs are sourced from the bottom row of the account mapping matrix.

When account mapping, your company's prospect list should be a huge population of companies that you are seeking some novel way to engage more deeply. You've probably had some light interaction with them, come across them in research, or have some other reason to suspect they're worth knowing. Now you're looking for ways to learn more and hopefully create a next step in their buying journey. ELG will deliver.

Mining prospect lists for qualified leads is often likened to finding a needle in a haystack. The lists are just too big to make harvesting leads from them practical with any playbook that doesn't scale automatically. This creates a Catch-22, however, because generic mass outreach is ineffective, yet manually personalizing or researching the accounts is too slow and costly.

The traditional solution is to pay third-party data brokers or data enrichment companies to add more dimensions of data to these prospect lists. These typically include firmographic data such as employee count or industry, which can help with the broad strokes of prospect qualification. It helps somewhat, but it's kind of like trying to catch rain with a fork.

ELG is a better way. Running your prospect list through the account mapping matrix with your partner ecosystem is akin to running a magnet along the haystack: it instantly shows you where all the needles are hiding.

Moreover, each match it finds comes with the benefit of context directly from your partners. Which prospects are customers, active sales targets, or even just prospects of your partners creates a rich profile around each account from which you can automate outreach, personalize messaging, and elevate from generic prospects to ecosystem-qualified leads.

Forget third-party data—this is **second-party data**. It's not the same lead lists or enrichment data that can be bought by anyone with a credit card. Quite the contrary, it's something that is unique and proprietary to you by virtue of the fact that it originated from your unique and proprietary ecosystem.

The output is a universe of rich, highly contextualized lead lists that can be marketed to in a way that's useful for everyone involved. Let's look at a few ways this methodology is used in the real world.

Marketing Automation and Account-Based Marketing

The classic tools of the trade for modern marketers are **marketing automation** and **account-based marketing (ABM)**. Both of these techniques rely on fortifying your target account lists with as much data and context as possible and then tailoring your outreach and messaging sequences to them based on that specific knowledge.

In the case of marketing automation, this is done with segments of prospects in the form of lists, and in the case of ABM, the personalization makes its way down to the company level and specific campaigns are built and launched company-by-company.

Ed Ceballos, head of partnerships at Everflow Technologies, has mastered the art of generating EQLs at scale and then using marketing automation to drive the sales pipeline. Ceballos runs an ELG playbook that spans both their marketing and sales organizations. Partner data flows in from their ecosystem via Crossbeam and then gets routed into HubSpot, where it is used for co-marketing, cross-selling, and analytics.

Like countless other companies, the Everflow partnerships team lived in spreadsheets before they discovered ELG. They spent months collecting and consolidating information from partners to get their co-marketing and co-selling gears in motion. This cost weeks of time and forced them to be overly selective about which campaigns they executed and with whom, limiting how much they could leverage their partner ecosystem for marketing motions.

"For any program to work, you have to design it to be scalable and replicable," says Ceballos. "Getting data from our partner ecosystem into HubSpot allows us to wrap everything up consistently, from identifying target accounts to executing marketing campaigns."

For example, Ceballos could build a report in Crossbeam identifying mutual prospects and refine the list using filters based on data he's bringing from HubSpot. The Crossbeam and HubSpot integration automatically creates a contact list in HubSpot from the report, simplifying targeting for co-marketing campaigns. Anytime new overlaps emerge in Crossbeam, they'll sync with the corresponding contact list in HubSpot (see Figure 14.3).

"Now when I agree to something with a partner, it's not like I'm throwing a hot potato to marketing; I'm just giving them the right data they need to execute," says Ceballos.

As it turns out, marketing automation with ELG is a fun and exciting evolution of a well-established practice. Once lists are loaded into your marketing automation platform, the applications of how they get used are

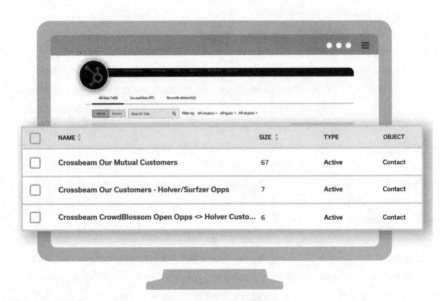

FIGURE 14.3 Dynamic co-marketing lists in HubSpot update automatically with data from Everflow's partner ecosystem.

only limited by your imagination and the rules of engagement you've established with your partners.

Here are some examples of tailored content that can be sent by marketing orgs to prospect lists. Each list would be made up of companies where ELG data enrichment revealed their shared connections to your ecosystem:

- Joint case studies showing how you and one or more partners have delivered a powerful joint value proposition to a shared customer;
- Links to white papers or documentation about specific integrations known to be relevant to the target list; and
- Invitations to joint webinars or other events for shared prospects.

Across the board, this kind of customized outreach is significantly more likely to drive open rates, clicks, and ultimately engagement with your marketing assets. This creates an engine through which prospects progress down your marketing funnel and qualify into sales conversations at a predictable pace and a higher conversion rate than you can achieve by other means.

Taken to its extreme, this process of targeting lists with personalized content leads you to the practice of ABM. In ABM, there are no longer lists but instead personalized strategies that are unique to the individual company being targeted.

ELG is an ABM superpower, as it offers compelling ways to further increase engagement with target accounts and increase their chances of engaging in your buying cycle. It not only allows you to make smarter choices about which accounts to include in an ABM campaign (ahem, EQLs, ahem) but also allows you to use rich second-party data to decide how to customize your campaign. In ABM campaigns, ELG data can be used to tailor targeted ads, personalized email outreach, account-specific events, social media engagement, personalized videos, and more.

The net effect of these strategies is that ELG serves as a force multiplier that can be overlaid on the tools and strategies your marketing team already has in place. It can dramatically increase your rate of conversion from prospects to qualified leads, be used for much more relevant personalization, and be validated by undeniable data about the connection between ecosystem connections and downstream performance.

Outbound: Upgrade Your SDRs to PDRs

We've already seen how the playbook of hiring sales development representatives (SDRs) to cold-call into lead lists is a dying game. It has reached a level of market saturation that has made the practice less effective and more expensive than ever, and few companies have the ingenuity to make it work for them economically.

So what are those few companies doing to make SDR outreach work in this environment? They're tossing the old "buy, spray, and pray" strategy to the curb and instead leveraging SDRs to conduct strategic, targeted, personalized outreach to the companies who are most likely to reply and engage.

ELG makes this playbook possible. In this demand generation playbook, we'll walk through how several companies are using ELG data and strategies to change the way outbound works at their companies.

In doing so, many companies are upgrading their SDR teams into teams of **partner development representatives** (**PDRs**). Whether donning that official title or not, these outbound opportunity generators have an ELG playbook through and through:

- Selecting and prioritizing target accounts based on signals from ELG data;
- Personalizing outreach and content to reflect where and how the target account is already engaged within the partner ecosystem;
- Leveraging partner relationships for introductions and "breakthrough events" that cause the target to engage;
- Tailoring first calls and demos to reflect the features, integrations, and known needs of the prospect based on ecosystem data; and
- Handing off the qualified opportunity to an account executive with a fully loaded dossier of ecosystem-informed context that saves time and preserves information.

With ELG overlaid on an SDR team, we experience an entirely new take on outbound that radically shifts the success rates and efficiency of the motion. The SDR mindset thus evolves to a more "quality over quantity"—or better yet "quality *and* quantity"—approach in which ecosystem intelligence and relationships are positioned to make SDR teams start working again.

Building a Qualified SDR Pipeline

Your SDR team should walk into every new conversation with confidence and context—not sweaty palms and a generic demo. Just ask Sylvain Giuliani, head of growth and operations at Census, a reverse ETL platform. His preferred ELG playbook involves surfacing sales intelligence from Census's tech partners to find pockets of untapped demand that might exist in their partner ecosystem and then parlaying that knowledge into SDR plays to bring those leads to life. It's a perpetual motion machine of new activities and insights that keep the sales pipeline populated.

Giuliani first builds reports in Crossbeam to compare the enormous pool of Census's target accounts against his partners' customers. If partner(s) share data with Census, Giuliani configures his report columns to include fields such as account website, how the partner classifies the account in their customer relationship management (CRM) system (e.g. small, mid-market, or enterprise), the partner's account executive name, and the partner's account executive email.

The initial run is obviously a goldmine of account lists, targets, and quality contextual information that can be used to load up target lists for SDRs. What's equally exciting, however, is the way in which those lists continue to evolve and expand every single day.

By setting up notifications on these reports, Census can know the moment one of their prospects has a new piece of signal that reflects buying intent, an evolution in their tech stack, or a new messaging angle that might help open them up to a conversation.

"That's a strong compelling event for us to sell Census," says Giuliani. "It gives us an exclusive lens into a prospect's tech stack that we can't get anywhere else because it's powered by our partner ecosystem. You gain information that you can't scrape off a prospect's website or buy from a data enrichment service."

Those notifications allow Giuliani to receive an email alert personally, direct one to the appropriate sales leader, or feed one into an automated workflow. When appropriate, the Census team can engage the partner manager or the partner's account owner in a Slack Connect channel saying, "Hey, we just saw that you closed Acme Corporation. What's the state of the account? Do you think it's time for us to get into there? Do you know what your customer's strategy is to get all their data into your platform? Because we'd like to help accelerate that onboarding process."

This rich context—a mixture of data, timely events, and relationship context—all land on the desks of the SDR team to generate opportunities. From there, SDRs can spike conversion rates with hyper-personalization. Reps will personalize their outbound emails to highlight a "better together" story and embed relevant co-marketing materials (think: one-pagers, case studies, or demo videos) to support their messaging.

Here's an example of an email a Census SDR might send to a prospect named Jane at ACME Corporation. ACME Corporation is a customer of Census's partner, a marketing automation tool named Holver:

Hi Jane,

We're close partners of Holver here at Census, and I noticed that you own the Holver implementation in your role as Data Engineering Director at ACME.

Are there any user or company attributes living in your data warehouse that your teams would like to access in Holver to do deeper analysis?

We did this recently for our shared customer Saasco, who uses Census to pipe data from their warehouse into Holver. In their case, a "power user" was defined in their warehouse and synced to Holver using our Reverse ETL platform. Saasco's Product and Marketing teams can now do segmentation and analytics filtered by power user status, which has resulted in a huge uptick in their conversion rates. You can see the full case study here (link).

I suspect we could find similar opportunities in your data. Would you like to see a demo?

Best,
Esdee R.
Sales Development Representative

With this ELG playbook, Census can now put a process around its partnership motions. Its SDRs become de facto PDRs, leveraging ELG to find wins.

This is an extremely differentiated approach when compared to the kind of messaging personalization we've seen in previous generations of SDR strategy. We've all received that cold email that says, "I noticed that you're in the software industry too" or "We find that companies with 500 to 1000 employees really get value from our product."

These legacy personalizations based on third-party firmographic data are pale imitations of what you see here. In this case, the customization is deeply rooted in a value story, one rich enough to speak to not just the problems being solved by a given company's use of software but the specific software product itself. It's not self-serving or siloed in its messaging; it's an ecosystem story that conveys a different spirit of message and a different tone of how your team seeks to create value for this prospect. It's indicative of a new era of outbound.

Automating Targeted SDR Sequences

Rob Simmons, vice president of sales at LeanData, tells us that his company's outbound playbook has also been rewritten with ELG at its core. By running ELG plays at every stage of their funnel, the LeanData team grew partner-influenced revenue from 3% to 80% in a year. A crucial part of that evolution was making sure their SDR team was running plays powered by data and relationships from the company's partner ecosystem.

"Normal outbound is noisy and everyone gets a ton of it. Leveraging partner ecosystem data to understand a prospect's tech stack and custom tailor your pitch accordingly gives your reps a huge advantage," says Simmons.

Hitting the right prospect at the right time with the right message is absolutely critical.

Now, SDRs are using partner data to craft more personalized and targeted messaging about LeanData and its integrations. "Our SDRs are using Crossbeam data to send different email sequences to our partners' customers and highlight our joint value messaging," says Simmons.

SDRs will look at the Crossbeam Salesforce widget on an account to quickly see which partners also have relationships there (see Figure 14.4). Simmons has taught SDRs to "view details" about an overlap in the Salesforce widget. This way, they can see when an account became a customer of an integration partner and determine the best time to connect with the account on a given integration.

"Every two months, our partner team gets in front of our SDRs and does a recap of ELG best practices to maximize their pipeline. Repetition is key to transition partners into a subconscious part of their sales motion," says Simmons.

The SDRs have email sequences specific to each integration partner in their **sales engagement platform**. When an SDR sees a target account that

FIGURE 14.4 SDR view of ecosystem overlaps in Salesforce.

overlaps with a partner's customer, they'll enroll those contacts in that specific sequence. The LeanData partnerships team doesn't auto-enroll contacts in a sequence because they want their SDRs to review the overlaps to make sure there aren't conflicts with existing email sequences scheduled in their sales engagement platform.

The email sequence is made of a few emails that introduce LeanData, their integration with the integration partner, and the joint value of the integration. "I'm a big believer in this play for SDRs. I think about how much outreach I personally get, and the stuff that catches my eye is either highly personalized and/or it mentions a tool that I'm already using," says Simmons.

Reinventing Event Strategy

No matter what the world throws at it, event marketing just can't be stopped. Innovations in teleconferencing, rampant cost cutting, and even a global pandemic would seem like a good recipe for the death of the conference.

Yet the events industry continues to thrive, with many industry conferences now breaking their pre-pandemic attendance records.

Like most things that don't die, however, events certainly have a way of evolving. Iconic technology brands such as Gainsight—the world's leading SaaS customer success platform—are shaping what world-class event strategy looks like in the modern era.

"Our Pulse conference is one the best and most important things we ever built," Gainsight CEO Nick Mehta told me in a recent conversation. "It's our annual opportunity to live out our company values with an incredible ecosystem of our customers, partners, and team."

Pulse, presented by Gainsight, has become a juggernaut. Over the last 10 years, Pulse has been home to more than 5,500 in-person attendees and more than 20 thousand virtual attendees spanning six continents and attracting professionals from all industries and levels—from recent college graduates to executives of Fortune 500 companies, including GE, Microsoft, Cisco, and Salesforce.

How does Gainsight ensure that its ecosystem of stakeholders gets the most value possible from Pulse without violating community trust? With ecosystem-led growth playbooks, of course!

In the old days, event managers had to make an impossible choice: share attendee lists and enable mass connection-making, or keep attendee lists private and strip away the on-site value to partners and sponsors. Gainsight always puts attendees first in this situation. "The trust of our attendees is paramount," says Mike Barnes, Gainsight's head of ISV (independent software vendor) and tech partnerships. "But yes, we also want to make sure that our partners and sponsors can connect with interested attendees to make sure both sides get the information they need from the event."

These potentially opposing goals turn out to be a beautiful use case for an ELG-style approach of modern account mapping. Using Crossbeam, Gainsight is able to match up the list of attending companies at Pulse with the target prospects, opportunities, and customers of all its partners and sponsors (see Figure 14.5).

From there, it has a finite, curated list of attendees that would represent extremely high value introductions for its partners and sponsors—no mass list sharing or shotgun approaches needed. Gainsight can then efficiently reach out to those attendees to ensure their opt-in to an intro (or collect a more general opt-in at registration) and make the most valuable connections happen with extremely tight controls on data privacy and trust.

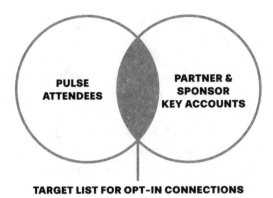

TARGET LIST FOR OPT-IN CONNECTIONS

FIGURE 14.5 Gainsight's ELG-driven attendee matchmaking.

"It's a goldmine for everyone—attendees especially," Barnes told me. "Think mass personalization of the event experience right down to the Gainsight partners they care about meeting on site. This is a much more specific, targeted, opt-in-oriented way to connect sponsors in our ecosystem to attendees."

Indeed, there is an increasing trend among conference organizers to offer this ELG-style account mapping exercise as a sponsor perk. Of course, only the sponsors who are using an ELG platform such as Crossbeam are able to partake, as it relies on the event connecting and list-building with the sponsor's sales pipeline and target prospect lists.

This playbook doesn't stop with big industry conferences either. Gainsight has found huge success running small, curated local dinners in the cities of its prospects. Many of these smaller events are run in conjunction with a local partner who knows the city and can offer up their network into the attendee mix.

"Curating the right folks in the room is a big exercise where it's extremely important to be thoughtful," Barnes told me. "There is an 'art of the possible' stage at the beginning of planning one of these, and lately we run an ELG play to do that work."

Barnes says there is an important chemistry to making a dinner valuable to guests and hosts alike. "Hosting a dinner with a partner means filling the room with the right mix—joint customers should love both products and use them together. There needs to be a good enough mix of customers and prospects to balance out the social proof with the potential upside of the dinner."

The resulting ideal breakdown is a stroke of brilliance (see Figure 14.6). Each side feels like a winner:

- For each host, 70% of attendees are sources of potential new business, and the other 30% is made up of their existing happy customers. It's a stacked room.
- Each host will interact with a pool of new ecosystem-qualified leads who already use a partner's product but not their own.
- The 20% made up of shared relationships is able to be curated to ensure the best possible representation of success stories without consuming too many seats.
- For each attendee, the dinner is perfectly split 50/50 between customers and prospects, keeping a healthy balance of knowledge and informed perspectives.

In a world without ELG and account mapping, this process would be a mess of data oversharing, confusing LinkedIn searches, and unpredictable outcomes. Instead, it can be done in a 30-minute prep call.

"These ELG playbooks allow us to be purposeful with our events, from the smallest to the largest," Mehta told me. "We can put our attendees first without creating other risks to the quality of their experience."

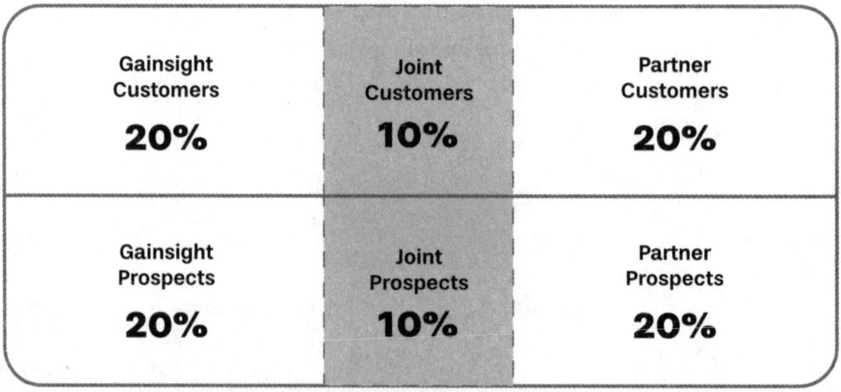

Gainsight Customers	Joint Customers	Partner Customers
20%	**10%**	**20%**
Gainsight Prospects	Joint Prospects	Partner Prospects
20%	**10%**	**20%**

FIGURE 14.6 Gainsight's target attendee makeup for co-hosted events.

Turning Investors into Pipeline Generation Engines

Any executive at a venture-backed company knows that, when it comes to investor value-add, mileage varies wildly. The best investors drop leads on your doorstep on a regular basis, but the vast majority need to be "pulled" into deals rather than pushing them to you automatically. This is especially true over the long term, as the honeymoon period of a new investment gives way to the often decade-long gauntlet of building an enduring company.

In recent years, however, venture capital, private equity, and crossover investment firms have looked to ecosystem-led growth as a new playbook for driving lead generation for their portfolio companies.

Investors are a unique breed of partner. You certainly win together and have highly aligned incentives. And while your product offerings couldn't be farther apart, it turns out that your ideal customer profile may overlap more than you think.

Investor relationship networks definitionally include the prospective customers and buyers in just about every space where they invest. These relationships are built in the course of due diligence and company research but can also be used selectively as qualified sales introductions. Put this all together and you've got a fascinating ELG play that is picking up steam in the investor community.

One such example is Okta Ventures, the venture capital arm of identity and access management powerhouse Okta. Okta Ventures has one of the most compelling portfolio value-add programs I've worked with. Much of that is due to the innovative approach taken by its leader Austin Arensberg.

Arensberg has gone all-in on ELG as a strategy for adding value to his portfolio companies. This was clear from day one of us working with him, as we watched Okta Ventures source 60 ecosystem-qualified leads for its portfolio companies in just its first two weeks running this playbook.

"Corporate venture capital organizations typically rely on one-time annual conferences or occasional virtual events to provide matchmaking for their portfolio companies. But we wanted to do matchmaking continuously and at a more granular level—and only an ELG playbook could power that engine," says Arensberg.

Now, Okta Ventures is working with its portfolio companies including DataGrail, a data privacy start-up, to scour its partnerships and customer relationships to help move the needle on DataGrail's existing deals. When companies such as DataGrail choose Okta Ventures, they don't just get an investor; they get the keys to one of the SaaS world's largest ecosystems— easily navigable thanks to ELG.

Arensberg and Daniel Barber, CEO at DataGrail, are reshaping how partner ecosystems are the next frontier of venture capital firms providing value to portfolio companies. The DataGrail/Okta integration helps chief information security officers identify which of their internal systems are exposing personally identifiable information so they can comply with privacy regulations. Chances are, a customer of Okta is a highly sought-after account for DataGrail.

Okta Ventures and DataGrail used a classic ELG account mapping matrix to instantly determine the following:

- How many of Okta's customers overlap with DataGrail's customers to explore cross-selling motions; and
- How many of Okta's customers overlap with DataGrail's open opportunities for Okta's sales team to broker warm introductions to specific stakeholders at an account for DataGrail or help DataGrail push their deals further down the funnel.

"What used to take two to three months of account mapping, long meetings, and manual processes now takes ten minutes," says Arensberg.

This playbook has also spared Barber and his team from administrative burden. "The CRM data is live and constantly updated. I don't have to be pulling data and then sending it over every week or every month," says Barber. "It's saving our team a couple of hours a week," he says.

After identifying 10 ecosystem-qualified leads in their first meeting, Okta Ventures' team is now helping DataGrail get in front of Okta's sales reps to accomplish the following:

- Gain insights about key decision-makers and the **procurement process** for strategic accounts;
- Identify opportunities to launch co-marketing and co-selling motions; and
- Request intros from Okta's sales reps to specific stakeholders at DataGrail's strategic accounts.

Now, Okta Ventures and DataGrail are actively collaborating to advance those ecosystem-qualified leads further down the sales funnel. Barber says knowing which prospects are customers of Okta helps DataGrail's account executives better frame the conversation on how DataGrail can add value.

Barber adds, "We can be a lot more thoughtful about the way we approach ecosystem deals or deals with Okta customers. This ELG playbook is all about providing that secure place but then also providing that framework for us to work together and a reminder that we should be hopping on a call, doing account mapping together, and having more active conversations."

The marketing funnel is perhaps the most dynamic and important piece of a company's growth strategy. It's responsible for generating the leads that become sales pipeline, and only that pipeline can turn into paying customers.

ELG changes the game for marketers, and in this chapter we've seen firsthand how marketing leaders, CEOs, and revenue operations teams are infusing ecosystem data and relationships to reinvent their traditional demand generation tactics.

The result: more pipeline that is more qualified and actionable than ever. Now we have to close that pipeline—so we head on to sales.

15 Ecosystem-Led Sales: Close Bigger, Better Customers Faster

This may be the most important chapter in this book, and that should come as no surprise. In Chapter 14, we explored how ELG-powered demand generation playbooks can deliver a new universe of ecosystem-qualified leads (EQLs) into the hands of your sellers. These EQLs, along with leads from other sources that can be prioritized and enriched using insights from your ecosystem, are the raw materials for a supercharged sales motion powered by ELG.

"To create real outcomes, we have to incorporate these ELG playbooks into the go-to-market practices of everybody in the revenue organization," says Sam Jacobs. He should know. A former chief revenue officer himself, Jacobs is now founder and CEO of Pavilion, an international community of sales, marketing, success, and RevOps leaders from the world's fastest-growing companies.

"Ecosystems are a unique and proprietary asset that can help companies grow and scale effectively," says Jacobs. "As existing playbooks continue to be disrupted by AI and other forces, they may be one of the only defensible paths to market in the future."

In this chapter, we'll explore how your company can elevate the role of your partner ecosystem in your sales strategy with the combination of sales intelligence, relationship pathways, and timely actionable insights. This will add up to a veritable "closing command center" for your sales team that creates demonstrably positive effects on your efficiency and revenue growth.

There's a reason why storied venture capital firm Andreessen Horowitz is willing to bet on companies that prioritize a partner-generated pipeline, rather than a direct sales-generated pipeline. An ecosystem-led growth approach for sales allows companies to do more without adding more people and partners.

"Partnerships are more important than ever," Sarah Wang, managing partner at Andreessen Horowitz, said onstage at the Supernode Conference in 2022. "You're bringing in pipeline, you're shortening sales cycles, and you're increasing conversion rates. That's a need-to-have, not a nice-to-have."

The stories in this section aren't just from partnership teams—they're from sales teams and senior executives at companies where ELG selling has taken a prominent role in their growth stories. Let's explore how a wide array of hypergrowth companies have employed the fruits of their partner ecosystems across strategies, tool sets, and existing playbooks to build something entirely new that changes the way their companies win and grow.

Strategy and Buy-In: The ELG Sales Tetrahedron

I love partnership professionals and the teams they lead. They've been our muses at Crossbeam, and many have become my close friends in the years I've spent working in this space. But it's important to be intellectually honest about the role that partnership professionals play in bringing an ELG strategy to your company: they are necessary, but not sufficient. Without the buy-in of your sales leadership and other executives, your ELG strategy will never reach escape velocity.

Fortunately, this is a problem with proven solutions. There are many shining examples of companies where senior leadership has chosen to invest in ecosystem-led growth. This results in a set of scalable, efficient sales playbooks that propel these companies into hypergrowth. Just look at Braze.

Braze is a leading customer engagement platform that powers interactions between consumers and brands they love. They went public in November 2021 and have offices across North America, Europe, and Asia-Pacific.

"Consistent revenue growth requires accelerants, and your partner ecosystem adds fuel to the sales fire," Myles Kleeger, president and chief commercial officer of Braze, told me recently.

Kleeger and the team at Braze have figured out how to apply sales thinking to partnerships, and their partner ecosystem has since had transformative effects on the shape and efficacy of their sales motions. "If you look under the hood at some of our most effective playbooks, you'll find that ecosystem-led growth is at the core," says Kleeger.

So what is Braze doing so well? Dave Goldstein knows it all. Goldstein has been with Braze for over a decade—having originally served as their very first salesperson, among other firsts—and now serves as vice president of Global Solutions Alliances. As you can imagine, he has seen their full journey to hypergrowth and has built up some incredible stories to tell along the way.

When Goldstein talks about bringing ELG to life inside of Braze, he pulls inspiration from his side job as a volunteer firefighter. "In firefighting, we talk about the fire tetrahedron," he explains. "For a fire to start, you need fuel, a source of heat, and oxygen—plus a chemical chain reaction that keeps it burning. Without all four, you've got no fire" (see Figure 15.1).

When it comes to rolling out ELG playbooks among the sellers at Braze, Goldstein has discovered that a similar tetrahedron is at work. The

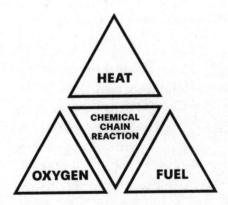

FIGURE 15.1 The fire tetrahedron.

FIGURE 15.2   The ELG sales tetrahedron.

elements of Goldstein's ELG sales tetrahedron (see Figure 15.2) include the following:

- **Tooling:** Get the partner data and tooling house in order;
- **Data:** Democratize the data and optimize everyone's time;
- **Buy-in:** Continue the important work of sales enablement and continue earning buy-in from leadership; and
- **Chain reaction:** At the center, a chain reaction of scalable systems and processes is the engine that makes ELG work inside of a sales organization.

Let's explore each of these components and the planning work required to bring them to life inside of your organization.

Tooling

Much of this book up to this point has provided the groundwork for solid tooling that establishes data connectivity among the members of your partner ecosystem and unlocks the opportunity to empower your sales team with that data.

Goldstein recalls a time before ELG platforms such as Crossbeam where this level of tooling was simply not available, and the process of account mapping and data discovery with partners was governed by spreadsheets and emails. Braze's adoption and rollout of Crossbeam among its ecosystem of partners allowed for a transformation that, in Goldstein's words, "got the partner tooling house in order" (see Figure 15.3).

> **GET PARTNER TOOLING AND DATA HOUSE IN ORDER**
>
> **BEFORE** → **AFTER**
>
> Disparate tools, inconsistent processes, minimal data refresh → Connected tools, consistent processes, data refresh
>
> Basic data, minimal insight to drive leadership buy-in → Treasure trove of data/analytics to support buy-in of ELS program
>
> Lack of security and governance → Security and governance controls

FIGURE 15.3 The ELG tetrahedron: tooling transformation.

Data

With the tools in place to unlock its ELG data layer, the next question for Braze was how to, in Goldstein's words, "democratize the data and optimize everyone's time." This is a critical piece of the ELG sales tetrahedron—while it may sound like it takes some control away from partner account managers (PAMs) in the organization, what it really does is radically improve their efficiency and impact.

Goldstein's point here is that getting a controlled, focused amount of data directly into the hands of sellers and sales leadership can drastically speed up the value creation process (see Figure 15.4).

We'll talk later in this chapter about the ways in which data makes its way into the hands of sellers—most notably by meeting them where they are via CRM integrations and analytics dashboards. This is true for Braze as well.

"The days of trying to chase every individual account and partner interaction down manually are over," Goldstein says. "Everything is in our sales CRM, and our sellers and sales leaders have access to it. We've flipped the model on its head, given sellers control of the process, and now they engage us when they need us—not the other way around."

Buy-In

The third piece of the tetrahedron is to never stop the important work of sales enablement and earning buy-in from leadership.

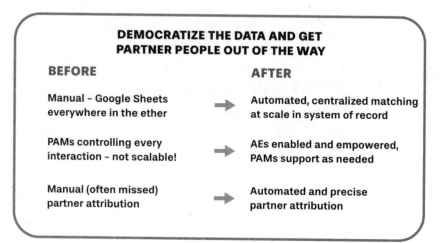

FIGURE 15.4 The ELG tetrahedron: democratize the data.

"I started in sales, and I can tell you with certainty that any new strategy has to be undeniable in its impact before it will be taken seriously," Goldstein told me. "So when we embark on the important step of bringing salespeople into the fold, we come armed with the data."

At Braze, the impact has been immense. For instance, Braze has seen that leveraging partners has resulted in a higher deal close rate, larger average deal size, and a powerful source of new pipeline generation.

"Put yourself in the shoes of a sales leader or seller and think about the kind of pipeline coverage you need in order to hit your goals," says Goldstein. "For the ecosystem to consistently help deliver that, at higher deal values and close rates, is profoundly impactful" (see Figure 15.5).

Here too, these practices come to life by sheer virtue of having the data in the right places accessible by the right people. This isn't the sole work of the partnership team—quite the contrary, it becomes part of the regular cadence of business in pipeline reviews, sales training sessions, SKOs, and more.

According to Goldstein, "The global sales leadership goes from the fringes to being firsthand advocates for ELG sales. They have reports where they can see the sellers who are falling behind when it comes to engaging the ecosystem to drive the best possible sales results." Indeed, with leadership buy-in, Goldstein shows how you tap into a virtuous cycle that connects training to performance to results and back again.

PERPETUAL ENABLEMENT AND BUY-IN

BEFORE		AFTER
Each partnerships person doing it their own way	→	Partnerships enabled on a consistent global process
Global sales leadership on the fringe, minimal enablement and support	→	Global sales leadership enabled to support top-down
AEs and BDRs exhibit rogue behavior due to lack of regular enablement	→	Regular cadence of enablement on globally consistent process (orientation, SKO, quarterly, etc.)

FIGURE 15.5 The ELG tetrahedron: enablement and buy-in.

Chain Reaction

As Goldstein learned in firefighting, when these sufficient conditions are met it takes just one spark to create a chain reaction that causes the fire to grow and grow. So too does ELG sales come to life and expand in a chain reaction once the conditions are met and the first wins are put on the board. ELG wins create more data, which leads to better training and more buy-in, more proliferation of tools, more wins, and so on.

"Set lofty goals and say them loudly," says Goldstein. "Create those reporting mechanisms to show how you're progressing toward those targets so sales leadership can see it in real time and come on the journey with you."

Michelle Geltman from Branch, whose lessons on goal alignment were covered in Chapter 9, runs a nearly identical playbook: seek leadership buy-in, align partnership goals with business goals, and implement the right tools (see Figure 15.6).

To me, it says something pretty profound that these two innovative companies each independently arrived at nearly identical strategies for rolling out ELG at their companies in a way that drives top-down support. It's a playbook that I endorse (whether you visualize it as a tetrahedron or a virtuous cycle), and I hope every person reading this book can embrace it as well.

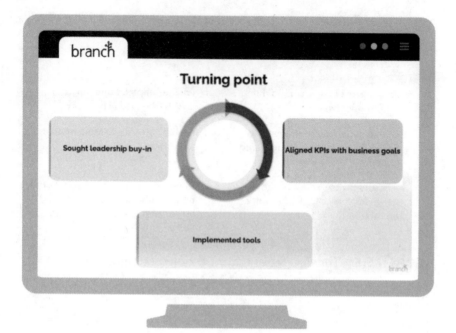

FIGURE 15.6 Branch slide from Supernode 2023.

The results at Branch have been staggering:

- 40% faster time to close;
- 44% increase in pipeline; and
- 50% increase in average deal size.

"This certainly didn't happen overnight," Geltman shared at the Supernode Conference in 2023, "but this is also not where Branch's story ends—there is so much more ahead."

In the remainder of this chapter, we'll meet many more leaders and hypergrowth companies whose stories echo those of the Braze and Branch teams. We'll go deep into the ways in which they build up the tools, systems, and processes to make ELG sales come to life at their companies.

Meeting Sellers Where They Are

In this section, we'll learn how ELG companies such as Fivetran and Intercom infuse the data and relationships from their partner ecosystems into the tools and systems that their sellers already use. A core tenet of ecosystem-led growth is that the data from the partner ecosystem must "pierce the veil" of partnership teams and make its way into the hands of those team members who interact with customers and prospects.

Perhaps no modern company understands this better than Fivetran. If you read Part I of this book, Fivetran's business model should sound familiar: their software automates the movement of data out of, into, and across cloud data platforms, eliminating the most time-consuming parts of the **extract, load, transform** (ELT) process so data engineers can focus on higher-impact projects.

Fivetran is a cornerstone of the modern data stack—so much so that their annual conference is called . . . well . . . the Modern Data Stack Conference ("MDSCon" for those in the know). Given the deeply integrated and collaborative nature of the companies in the modern data stack, it's no surprise that Fivetran has built its business on ecosystem-led growth motions. They have incorporated their partner ecosystem into every facet of their go-to-market model, in turn growing to over 5,000 customers and surpassing a $5 billion valuation.

CEO George Fraser, who cofounded Fivetran in 2012, isn't shy about their partner-centric mindset. "We are a partnership-driven company and always have been," he told me in a recent conversation. "Our second customer was a partner referral, and our partner ecosystem is just intrinsic to what we do. None of these tools do anything without data in them, and that's what Fivetran does—it feeds the data."

So how does this translate into playbooks and how does a co-selling powerhouse like Fivetran empower their sales reps to use ELG data? For that answer we can turn to Michael Bull, their director of strategic alliances, whose job is to translate Fivetran's strategic position in its ecosystem into value for their customers and growth plays for their sellers.

"We really are a true full stack consumer of ELG strategies," says Bull. "We do it all, from sales to CS and everywhere in between. But nothing happens if we don't get the data into the hands of our customer-facing teams."

What Bull and his team have constructed for their go-to-market counterparts is nothing short of a full-blown arsenal of ecosystem intelligence: insights embedded directly into the CRM, robust sales data models that blend ecosystem data with sales pipeline data, and rich integrations to their own internal analytics.

A starting principle behind their approach is to meet the sales team where they already are—in their Salesforce CRM system and Looker dashboards—rather than forcing the use of a new tool or needing to step out of existing workflows to access the data. To do this, they focused on three core touchpoints through which ELG data can make its way out of Crossbeam and into the hands of the sales team.

Touchpoint One: The Salesforce "Widget"

Sometimes you just need a dossier on a given account—and fast. Most sales reps who need such an at-a-glance look turn to their customer relationship management (CRM) system, which holds the basic facts and previous call notes about each prospective customer. But what if that dossier could tell you even more? What if, for an ecosystem-led company such as Fivetran, it could give you a comprehensive sense of where and how a company is wired into its partner ecosystem?

This kind of knowledge could inform the sales rep about which cloud destination is table stakes, which upstream integrations might matter most, or which agency partner has relationships with the account. This in turn could be used to customize a pitch, remove blockers from a deal process, or answer questions about client needs—thus bypassing or shortening what might otherwise be a time-consuming discovery and qualification process.

Whether sellers are doing prep work for a first call, working through a pipeline review with their managers, or simply getting sharp on the accounts in their book of business, they need an at-a-glance breakdown of ecosystem activity around any account at any time. For that, Fivetran has implemented a simple yet powerful Crossbeam widget directly inside of Salesforce (see Figure 15.7).

Yes, this is the same widget we saw other companies using to arm their SDR teams with context and data in the previous chapter about demand generation. As it turns out, this same data has powerful uses up and down the funnel. The widget provides sellers and their managers with zero-click visibility into partner overlaps right inside of the Account and Opportunity detail pages inside of Salesforce. Users can drill down into specific partner relationships in order to see more details, including information such as the sales rep or account manager who owns the relationship at the partner company.

Touchpoint Two: The Salesforce Data Model

If you give a mouse a cookie, he'll ask for a glass of milk.

FIGURE 15.7 The Crossbeam Salesforce widget (simulated data).

What happens after sellers get access to a CRM widget that lets them see ELG overlaps on individual accounts? They'll want to go bigger. Rather than simply looking up information about one account at a time ad hoc, they may want to view all the information at once for their entire territory, organize the data by different filters, and do exploratory analysis to discover where the greatest opportunities for partner collaboration might exist. This is the moment when sales teams go from reactive to proactive about ELG.

For this complex set of sales-related tasks, Fivetran loads all of their ELG account-mapping data directly into a custom object inside of Salesforce itself, making that data a first-class source of truth in the company's CRM data model. This process is accomplished using Crossbeam's native Salesforce integration, which does this **data mapping** and custom object creation automatically.

Bull shared a quote to this effect from Fivetran's own internal documentation: "Salesforce Reports are the best way to leverage [ELG account mapping] information—they let you see all overlaps, all overlaps for each population (my prospects, my opportunities, etc.), and also overlaps for highly targeted groups or filters of your choosing."

Data-savvy reps can build custom reports from scratch, but most consumers of this data simply tap into prebuilt reports that Bull's team has added into Salesforce—when a rep pulls one up, it's automatically tailored to only show a version of the report narrowed down to their own accounts.

Unsurprisingly, the most popular prebuilt reports harken back to the original concept of the account mapping matrix. They provide sellers with detailed rundowns of how accounts at various stages in their pipeline overlap with the customers and pipelines of their key partners:

- My Accounts vs Modern Data Stack Partner Customers;
- My Accounts vs Modern Data Stack Partner Opportunities;
- My Opportunities vs Modern Data Stack Partner Customers;
- My Opportunities vs Modern Data Stack Partner Opportunities;
- My Opportunities vs System Integrator Partner Opportunities; and
- My Opportunities vs System Integrator Partner Customers.

Sales managers have dashboards powered by this data too. They can see how each of their reps is performing with accounts shared with different key partners. They can track key activities with partners, which are also logged in the CRM. And they can diagnose deals that are slowing down or at risk through the lens of the ecosystem, often finding pathways to unstick an opportunity with the aid of a key partner.

Fivetran **business development reps (BDRs)**, whose job is to generate new pipelines, also have their own reports akin to the ones mentioned in the chapter about demand generation. So do **customer success managers**, who use reports such as "Upcoming Renewals with Overlaps" to inform renewal strategy. (More on these tactics later on as we move down-funnel with our ELG playbooks.)

Touchpoint Three: Analytics Dashboards

What happens after you give that mouse a glass of milk? Maybe he'll want to build a modern business intelligence dashboard to determine where the next cookie is coming from.

That's what Fivetran did. If you zoom out one click wider than their Salesforce CRM, you'll find Fivetran's data warehouse—a central source of truth that incorporates data from sales, marketing, product, finance, and operations to create a true nerve center of the company. Fivetran puts their ELG data there too.

Employees at Fivetran are extremely data driven, and as such they have access to powerful Looker dashboards that are driven by this underlying data warehouse. These dashboards contain comprehensive cross-functional data that may be useful in their work. For salespeople, that's a highly flexible and powerful lens into "partner engagement."

One such report isn't about individual accounts so much as it is about individual humans. Specifically, the salespeople's counterparts at partner companies. The "AE playbook" dashboard contains a special section powered by ELG data that lets each account executive at Fivetran see which account executives at partner companies share the most accounts in common with them. In other words, it tells them which partner sales reps are doing the same work as them at the same time—often with dozens of the same companies or more!

As it turns out, the commonplace structure of territories and goals among companies in the modern data stack makes it such that extremely high "rep to rep" overlap is quite common. And while there may be hundreds or thousands of sales reps across all of their partner companies, this dashboard allows each of Fivetran's reps to know which ones are worth investing the time and energy into relationship building.

In total, these three ELG touchpoints provide Fivetran's revenue organization with a robust and comprehensive set of jumping-off points for leveraging their partner ecosystem and relationships to create wins. Getting the right data in the hands of sellers and their managers without forcing them to use new tools or systems means that ELG strategies can become default playbooks used in the everyday management of growth and selling.

Of course, Fivetran's playbooks aren't the only ones that allow sellers to use existing channels to infuse ELG into their deals. Catherine Brodigan at Intercom has found similar success using a fourth touchpoint: Slack.

Bonus Touchpoint: Slack

My conversation with Catherine Brodigan at Intercom extended into sales team touchpoints as well and offers a powerful addition to those offered by Fivetran. To ensure her team doesn't miss a beat on driving partner attachment, Brodigan has rolled out two additional plays that leverage

Slack: custom alerts and a partnerships request channel. These two processes constitute a push and pull strategy for increasing partner attach rates, and neither could exist without ELG data and workflows.

Slack Alerts (Push Strategy)

As soon as an opportunity in Salesforce hits the "Solution Review" sales stage, the partner manager will get an alert in a Slack channel called #*no-partner-attached*. A "Solution Review" stage is assigned when the discovery call is completed, value drivers are identified, the champion is identified, and success metrics are defined.

The Slack alert includes the name of the account, the account owner, the sales region, the ARR amount, and a button to view the opportunity in Salesforce. Brodigan says, "The first thing that my team will do is look at the Crossbeam overlaps for that deal and then talk to the rep and say 'Hey, I notice there isn't a partner attached to this deal. What do you need from partner A, B, and C to help progress this deal?'"

Partnership Request Slack Channel (Pull Strategy)

Brodigan created a #partnership-requests Slack channel so that reps have a single place to go to get assistance on deals.

Perhaps a rep needs to get in front of a key stakeholder or decision-maker at an account, or maybe they need intel from a partner about an account's procurement and negotiation process. It's like their own personal help line. Reps simply need to complete a "Request Partner Intro" form in Slack with information about the account they need assistance with, what kind of partner they need help from (app or service), and how they'd like to work with that partner.

The partner manager will review each request as it comes in and then intro the rep to the partner in a Slack Connect channel with the partner. From there, Intercom's partner manager can brief their partner on the deal and the account and together, both partners can align on next steps.

Brodigan and her team encourage and remind reps to use this channel in onboarding sessions for new hires and as part of ongoing enablement for the sales team. Additionally, if reps direct message (DM) partner managers with these types of requests in Slack, they are actively encouraged to drop their request in that channel instead to create broader visibility.

Co-Selling

It's clear so far that sales teams can derive value from ELG data alone: account prioritization, customized messaging, targeted use of sales collateral, and reporting on wins are all ways that sales leaders and sellers can turn ELG data into better outcomes.

Sometimes, though, you want more than just data and context from your ecosystem. Actively engaging a partner to assist with a deal is a knockout punch that can push a deal forward, edge out competitors, and speed up a win. This is the art of co-selling.

The most successful ELG companies have built up co-selling as the main revenue driver for their companies, and we'll get to know several of them in this section. In short, **co-selling** means selling together. It's a natural extension of the "winning together" mantra of partnerships, and it happens any time sellers work directly with individuals at partner companies to generate leads, convert new customers, and grow existing accounts.

"The most important playbook in ecosystem-led growth is the co-selling playbook," Henry Patel, chief strategy officer at Jamf, told me in a recent conversation. Jamf is a cybersecurity software company whose products are used by over 71,000 organizations to manage and protect the devices, data, and applications used by their end users without getting in the way of the intended Apple experience. They have been public on Nasdaq since 2020.

A career revenue leader, Patel built his career at Jamf rising up through the sales organization. "Where, why, and how your partner ecosystem is leveraged in the selling process can be the difference between a linear trajectory and hypergrowth. The smartest sales leaders have figured this out, and they're running these ELG playbooks as a way of life."

Co-selling is the playbook where the indirect influence of your partner ecosystem turns into direct, attributable sales outcomes. In these cases, there is consistent and indisputable evidence that deals close even faster, the win rates are even higher, the contract values are even larger, and the long-term retention is even stronger.

This works for technology and channel partners alike, although the joint value story can vary from case to case. As long as there is a fundamental truth around customers being more successful when your products or services are combined, there is an intrinsic motivation for co-selling to take place.

In the account mapping matrix, this is the work typically done when one company's opportunity intersects with the opportunities or customers of a partner's:

- **Joint opportunity:** Co-sell together in pursuit of a joint win where your products make up a "better together" value proposition.
- **Your opportunity is a partner's customer:** Leverage partner intelligence, relationships, and advice to increase your speed and chances of winning a deal in your pipeline.
- **Your customer is a partner's opportunity:** Return the favor. Help partners cross-sell into your customer base, increasing feature adoption and making your existing clients "stickier" thanks to the "better together" value story.

In order to co-sell, you and your partner have to achieve alignment and take action. The steps here are easy:

- Discover the key people ("deal teams") on each side of the partnership.
- Open up a communication channel between those people.
- Establish and take a next best action that aligns with everyone's incentives.
- Measure and attribute the results.

Let's explore each of these steps as they come to life inside real companies and drive real outcomes (see Figure 15.8).

Find the Deal Team

This may sound like a trivial exercise, but it's perhaps one of the most complex parts of the traditional account-mapping motion.

If my company has 100 sales reps and your company has 100 sales reps, there are 10,000 potential ways in which one of my reps and one of yours could be attached to a given deal. Now add in territory reassignments and changing ownership. Now add in rep churn and new hires.

I know I said that my love language is 2 × 2 matrices, but 100 × 100 matrices are the stuff of my nightmares. The mere prospect of figuring out who "owns" a deal on each side of a partnership could be enough to cause some teams to throw in the towel.

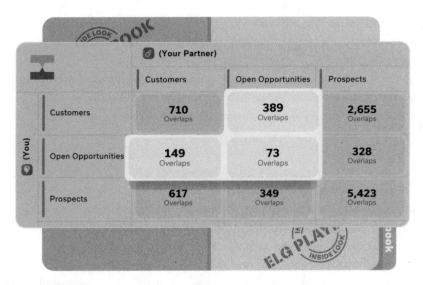

FIGURE 15.8 The account mapping matrix: co-selling.

ELG platforms solve this problem with ease, providing each side with an always-current lens into how accounts are owned at each of their partner organizations (assuming the partner shares this data, which is typically the case). With a map of "who owns what" inside of your partner's company, there are several ways to identify pairs of account owners who should collaborate:

- **Deal-specific alignment:** When reps, sales leaders, or partnership leaders are seeking partner assistance on a specific deal, they can identify the key deal team on the partner side instantly.
- **Opportunistic expansion:** When a rep has an existing relationship at a partner company or is already planning to have a meeting with a specific partner rep, they can easily run a report to view all of the deals they share. Why collaborate on one deal when it turns out you have 10 in common?
- **Alignment by best pairs:** Run a report to look at every possible combination of sales reps between you and a partner company. (Yes, all 10,000.) Sort by overlap count and identify the handful where there are the most overlapping opportunities. Proactively set up a collaboration call between these pairs to discover potential co-selling opportunities in high volumes and increase the odds of a fruitful outcome.

Depending on the maturity of your company and your dynamic with your partners, it may be the partner team or the sellers themselves who do this work.

I'm a huge proponent of training reps, setting clear expectations, and then letting them self-serve rep-to-rep connections. However, it's quite common that the partnership teams in such an exchange act as a go-between for these kinds of connections at first.

Open Up a Communication Channel

The net result of the previous exercises is that the right humans connect with each other via a communication channel. Choosing the right channel is critical.

E-mails, text messages, and other legacy communication channels are an easy pathway that have the advantage of being universal and simple. You can always go down that path, although it has some drawbacks. When we reach the "measure and attribute" later, for example, the haphazard nature of these kinds of communications can be troublesome.

We're about to learn a lot from Kris Lengieza, vice president of global partnerships and alliances at Procore Technologies. Procore is a leader in construction management software, where Lengieza has rolled out an enormously successful co-selling program. We'll share his end-to-end playbook in the remainder of this chapter, starting with his approach to opening up communications between partner deal teams.

Procore uses the communications tool Slack as the default channel for communicating with partners. (Microsoft Teams is another popular platform in this space where the same playbooks can be run.) In co-selling, fast and easy introductions to partner peers are key to keeping deals moving. So once the Procore sales rep knows who the partner's rep is, they'll connect with them in a Slack Connect channel. Such channels allow for messages to be sent in private chat rooms across company lines.

ELG platforms such as Crossbeam offer seamless Slack integrations that allow for data discovery and message tracking directly within Slack—again, meeting the reps where they already are.

"You go right into the Slack Connect channel with that partner, you request that person to be added if they're not already there, and then you can collaborate right there or even via a direct message," says Lengieza.

If there isn't a Slack Connect channel already, the Procore partner manager will spin one up and invite Procore's sales rep and the partner's sales rep (and whoever else needs to join the discussion) to the channel. That starts the rep-to-rep co-selling conversation, which usually continues through separate DMs or via follow-up conference calls.

When a sales rep wants to enlist a partner on a deal, the days of manual lookups and gatekeeping partner managers are gone. Lengieza says, "Now it's like, 'Yeah, we've got a significant number of our partners on Crossbeam, so we'll start there.' We'll usually have some pretty good hits on what we find there, and we can basically step out of the way and be a better partner to the sales team."

Align Incentives and Take Action

Once you're on the line with a willing partner, there is a cascade of ways in which the partner can take action to assist you in a deal. These vary quite a bit in the level of effort and strength of partnership required:

- Learning more about your solution and joint value proposition to ensure it gets included opportunistically whenever possible in their interactions.
- Sharing intelligence about the target opportunity's needs, tech stack, key decision-makers, procurement process, etc.
- Directly reaching out to the opportunity as a backchannel reference, making an endorsement of your product and reinforcing the "better together" story that makes your product the smart decision.
- Directly aiding in the sale of your product by incorporating it into their own sales pitch (if it's their prospect too), a customer success call (if it's their customer), or other touchpoint with the account.

Incentives matter a lot here. Some go-to-market professionals react to these potential actions with an understandable, "Why would I do that?" In the end, it's all about that "winning together" motivation.

Census knows how it's done. We last heard from Sylvain Giuliani at Census when we learned about how he uses ELG data to make his SDR team more effective. As head of growth and operations, his mandate extends down into the sales funnel as well. He offers some powerful insights into specific co-selling actions that allow partners to influence deals and create powerful outcomes on both sides.

It's a well-known and established understanding in the Census partner ecosystem that enabling integrations between Census and other tools makes both tools stickier, creates more value for customers, and increases customer lifetime value for both companies over time. (More on how that data gets calculated is coming up.) In other words, both Census and their partners are intrinsically motivated to increase the overlap in their customer bases.

So when the Census team has a strategic deal in flight, they look up the account in Crossbeam to see if any tech partners have an existing relationship. "It's like 'OK, cool. This customer is also using these technologies," says Giuliani. He then contacts those technology partners and their reps to gather information like the following:

- How does that prospect buy software?
- What was the procurement process like?
- How did you approach pricing negotiations?
- Can you share any information about your experience that might help us navigate this deal?

Giuliani says, "These kinds of conversations give us the intel to avoid hurdles in the sales process. The only people who have that information are the ones who've experienced the pain, which are people who have sold products to that organization before." Giuliani will share this information with his sales team to keep deals moving or prepare them for any unforeseen "gotchas" that might derail a deal. Perhaps the prospect has a strict data governance policy to be aware of, or maybe there's a difficult decision-maker they need to win over.

"It's that type of confidence where we know we're winning or we'll know we're losing very quickly," says Giuliani. For example, a prospect might share with a partner that they're not interested in purchasing Census for another six months. That information is just as valuable because then Census's sales team can adjust their sales forecast and re-prioritize which deals they focus on. "That's why running an ELG play through our ecosystem of partners is 10x more valuable than a shot in the dark on social media with a first- or second-degree connection," he says.

If a partner has strong relationships at a strategic account, Giuliani will ask them to put in a good word for the Census team. The partner might contact the prospect and say "Hey, I heard you've been thinking about using Census. We work with them all the time. They are a great tool and we highly recommend them." A simple message like that is all it takes to push a deal over the finish line or edge out a competitor.

"Having sales intel from our partner ecosystem allows us to be more in control of a deal. This means we can be more confident in the value story we're delivering and don't have to anchor ourselves to a lower contract value," says Giuliani. That kind of confidence results in 34% higher **annual contract values (ACVs)** on partner-influenced deals versus non-influenced deals for Census.

For some companies, incentives can be further enhanced by doing things that make the partners look good or allow them to "come bearing gifts" when directly co-selling to shared opportunities.

Alexis Petrichos, director of strategic partnerships and ecosystem marketing at Chili Piper, has rolled out a system of "partner vouchers" that help accomplish this goal. "Chili Piper is a strictly 'no discount' company," he told me. "But in cases where we have an open sales opportunity that is already an existing customer of our partner, we wanted to create a good motivation for our partners, endorse us and create urgency around the purchase."

The partner vouchers allow partners to provide some initial discount on Chili Piper to their customer, making the partner look like a hero and sealing the deal with the customer. The results of this program have been miraculous for Petrichos and his team:

- 2x the average contract value (ACV);
- A 90% close rate; and
- Half the sales cycle length.

At the end of the day, finding the collaborative "play" that you and your partner can agree to on a given account is an important dance that can happen at the company strategic level or even on a rep-to-rep relationship basis. But the key is clarity, consistency, and developing a cadence of making these actions happen. Then you just have to measure the results.

Measure the Results

We talked extensively about attribution, key performance indicators, and overcoming the partner paradox earlier in this book. The appropriate tracking and reporting on co-selling activity is one of the most critical places where this work gets done.

Many companies will use attribution tracking and reporting features directly inside of their ELG platform such as Crossbeam to keep tabs on partner influence and impact. Others, such as the Procore team led by Kris Lengieza, build this tracking directly into their CRM.

To tag a partner on a Salesforce account or opportunity, Procore uses the Salesforce Partner Object, enabling them to tag many partners on an account as many deals have multiple partners involved. "We can have a lot of partners on any one account, and we want to get as many partners as possible involved."

In addition to tracking attribution in Salesforce, the Procore team also built executive dashboards to keep a close eye on pipeline and metrics such as win rates on partner-influenced deals and partner attach rate. Procore does this by sending ecosystem and attribution from Crossbeam and Salesforce to its data warehouse, which powers data visualizations and dashboards in Tableau, its business intelligence platform.

Using a combination of Salesforce reports and executive dashboards in Tableau, Procore's partnership and sales leaders get more visibility into the pipeline and can use insights to do many things:

- **Analyze Partners' Overall Impact on the Business**
  Procore also conducts win/loss analyses to calculate sales velocity metrics on deals that are partner-sourced vs no partner involvement. "Then you can tell which partners have really helped the team win deals," says Lengieza. "Like, 'We don't lose when [Partner X] is involved.'"
- **Identify Which Partners Are Sourcing the Most Revenue**
  Procore will run reports to see which partners have sourced the most deals. That sparks discussions about how Procore can double down on those partnerships and invest in more co-selling and co-marketing opportunities with those partners.
- **Determine Which Partners Are Taking but Not Giving**
  Procore can see when they've sent partners a lot of leads and it isn't being reciprocated. The team will share this information with the respective partner manager so they can address it directly with their counterpart.

- **Manage Compensation Plans for Partner Managers**
  Procore will run reports to see which partner managers are bringing in the most partner-sourced revenue (after all, the partner managers' compensation depends on it!).

When it comes to sales velocity, Lengieza uses Crossbeam and Salesforce data in Tableau to measure three metrics:

- Days to close;
- Average sales price; and
- Win rate.

"As you can imagine, for partner-sourced deals, all the deal velocity metrics have improved," says Lengieza. He adds, "The cool thing about it is not just one of those sales velocity metrics improves and then the equation gets better—all the metrics improve. So then the equation gets a lot better because [customers] come to a decision quicker because they have the consensus of people they trust from the partners. They're more confident in what they're purchasing. So they're going to buy more products and not feel as though they need to negotiate as much, [because] they're getting value. The average sales prices are higher, and the win rates are higher, as well, because of that confidence."

Hyperscaler Cloud Marketplaces

Nowhere in this book have we named a specific company that your business should pursue as a partner. That's by design: each company's ecosystem is unique, and there is no such thing as a partner that would make sense for everyone. If that were true, all those "ecosystem development" playbooks would be unnecessary.

But there is one potential exception that is relevant to just about every company that transacts on or adjacent to the cloud: hyperscaler marketplaces.

As a refresher, a **hyperscaler** is a massive company such as Amazon, Google, or Microsoft that is aggressively investing to dominate the public cloud infrastructure market as well as the economies and marketplaces enabled by it.

Hyperscaler marketplaces are like supercharged B2B "app stores" where customers of these hyperscalers can also buy other products such as SaaS tools or professional services.

There is a vicious land grab happening between the three largest hyperscaler marketplaces, where Amazon Web Services (AWS) Marketplace, Google Cloud Platform (GCP) Marketplace, and the Microsoft Azure Marketplace are aggressively competing to attract both buyers and sellers. This makes for very attractive conditions for companies that want to sell on those marketplaces and gain access to the massive customer bases of the hyperscalers—and the smartest ones are taking full advantage.

According to the 2022 State of Cloud Marketplaces report from marketplace technology vendor Tackle.io, cloud marketplaces will exceed $10 billion in throughput by the end of 2023 and $50 billion by the end of 2025. They also found that 83% of technology sellers were planning to put more or significantly more focus and investment on marketplace as part of a cloud go-to-market strategy in the coming year.

From the perspective of a seller, a hyperscaler marketplace can offer you major perks, including:

- Simplified procurement processes where prospective customers purchase your product via existing agreements with the hyperscaler rather than directly via painfully negotiated agreements with you.
- Allowing your customer to access budget dollars at their company that would otherwise be out of reach. Budgets for hyperscaler cloud spend typically exist at the enterprise level and wouldn't otherwise be used for department-level technology purchases.
- Having the purchase of your product help "spend down" commitments your customer has made to the hyperscaler. Buyers make these spending commitments to access discounts and special perks but often find themselves with unspent dollars at the end of a contract term. This creates urgency and makes your product feel almost like a freebie that is paid for with committed spend that has to be consumed anyway.
- Co-selling benefits in which the sales representatives from the hyperscaler assist in selling your product into their customer base via the marketplace.
- As with all good marketplaces, a place for new customers to discover your offering.

From the hyperscaler perspective, having a dominant marketplace gives them the keys to the kingdom. At scale, a dominant hyperscaler marketplace would become the traffic cop for the entire cloud economy. It could create massive structural lock-in for its customers by intertwining economic commitments and contracts with multiple critical vendors.

The hyperscalers also take a commission on each transaction, which ranges from 5% to 10% in most cases at the time of publishing. It's a small cost for the vendors but drops right to the bottom line (at scale) for the hyperscalers. Talk about winning together.

So how does this all fit into ELG? Well, it's a specific but increasingly influential corner of the ecosystem where everything we've learned can be a force multiplier of your success: The playbooks you pursue around co-selling, accelerating deals, measuring the value of partner influence, and enabling your team can also apply to your hyperscaler marketplace partnerships. It just so happens that the partner in this case is one of the largest technology companies in the world—and the connective tissue between you and them is more transactional than technical.

The raw motion of account mapping is supported in some form by every one of these hyperscaler marketplaces. Some use modern ELG platforms such as Crossbeam, while others use more traditional PRM-style lead registration processes. But with enough elbow grease, you can tease out the intersection between your pipeline and the companies in these marketplaces.

From there, you can overlay the best practices in this book to get the most out of your rep-to-rep alignment, intelligence sharing, customized messaging, success measurement, and more.

The biggest hurdle is the act of getting listed on these marketplaces, maintaining that listing, and following each hyperscaler's specific processes for deal management. It can be a lot to take on, and a whole field of vendors have stepped in to offer technology and services that handle it for you. Tackle.io, WorkSpan, Suger, and Clazar are just a few of the players who can aid you along the hyperscaler marketplace journey.

Training, Enablement, and Accountability

Like Braze, the formula at Procore is to make sure the partner ecosystem is a useful partner to the sales team—not a blocker. Lengieza achieves this by consistently doing work to make sure sellers and their managers have the training and resources they need in order to help them qualify, advance, and close deals.

Here are some of the key pieces of the Procore playbook for making sure internal sales teams stay educated, motivated, and always up to date with the best way to run ELG.

Share Internal Stories About Partnership Wins

Lengieza includes partner-win stories in product and sales training sessions, and sometimes even company all-hands meetings. For example, Lengieza hosted a training for Procore's sales team on how to sell financial products with their enterprise resource planning (ERP) partners. "We talked about three case studies of how we were successful to either sell a connector we built, sell something a partner built, or work with a partner to build a custom integration. . . . We make sure those win stories show every step of the process: finding overlaps in the ELG data from Crossbeam, connecting with those partners, gathering intel and intros, and better navigating the sales process as a result," says Lengieza.

Participation in Forecast and Deal Calls

Partner managers regularly join forecast and deal calls to get sales updates and hold reps accountable to use partners. When reps share they're having a hard time with a particular account, partner team members will pull up Crossbeam for Salesforce to see which partners are on that account and check with the rep if they've talked to any partners.

"That has been the best way because there's public accountability," says Lengieza. "We tell them, 'We can help you with this. You could have leveraged these partners and that data was right there in Salesforce; you just ignored it.'" He adds, "It helps them, and then everyone else in that forecast call sees, 'Oh, that actually works.'"

Make Partners a Part of Your Weekly Sales Team Trainings

Lengieza says, "We're incorporating partners in all our trainings moving forward." Procore's partnerships team hosts weekly training sessions for the sales team, making sure partnerships are incorporated in each session.

For example, they might host a training on "How to Self-Source Pipeline" during which they'll review how to use ELG data from Crossbeam and how to see which accounts partners are attached to. They also host a weekly "Partner of the Week" training, where Procore invites partners to present to Procore's sales and customer success teams.

When leadership teams think about sales efficiency, they can't help but also think about accountability. These playbooks matter most when the outcomes can be measured, and that doesn't just happen when the deals close—it's also about making sure that every rep is putting the available plays to work when they present themselves.

Democratize the Data

Back at LeanData, Derek Safko, director of partnerships, runs a similar playbook that makes sure sales leadership is the tip of the spear for ELG success. "We've seen the value of bringing partners into deals, time and time again. Whether it be to salvage an at-risk deal or a customer that's likely to churn," says Safko.

To enable their sales teams, LeanData's partnerships team has built customized ecosystem-led growth dashboards for their AEs, SDRs, and customer success teams by sending partner data from Crossbeam into a Salesforce Custom Object. "When it comes to account selection and prioritization for our AEs and SDRs, we reference these ELG dashboards to make sure we're working accounts that already use our partners' products. We want to make sure we're actively reaching out to those accounts with that '1+1=3' story," says Safko. "It's important for sales leadership to play an active role in learning these dashboards and reports and incorporating the data into their team's motions."

To hold teams accountable, the partner team has biweekly calls with every AE. During these calls, the partner team will review an AE's current deals and compare them against the AE's personalized dashboard in Salesforce. See Figure 15.9 and note these dashboard details:

- The number of overlap counts with LeanData's top 10 integration partners;
- LeanData's top prospects without open opportunities, ranked by overlap volume; and
- LeanData's top prospects currently in pipeline, ranked by overlap volume.

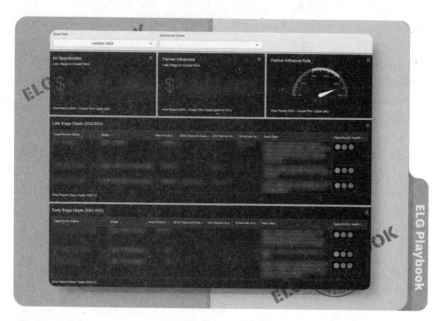

FIGURE 15.9 LeanData's ELG dashboard view (data redacted).

If the AE has an open opportunity that is stalled, they can use the dashboard to identify a few different tactics to get the deal back on track, including:

- Surfacing relevant integrations and "better together" solutions that can add more value to the deal;
- Identifying partners who can share intel about previous experiences with negotiations and procurement processes at the account; and
- Identifying partners who can potentially introduce the AE to the right stakeholders or decision-makers at the account.

"I'm responsible for driving a revenue number, and there are a lot of deals that get stuck for various reasons. Being able to leverage our partner ecosystem during these sales cycles really keeps the momentum going for these deals," says Rob Simmons, vice president of sales.

AEs and SDRs use partner dashboards to prioritize the accounts and partnerships they pursue based on the volume of overlaps that exist. For example, if a target account overlaps with multiple integration partners' customers, that account will likely be high on the priority list for the assigned reps. In LeanData's first year with running their ELG playbooks, partner-influenced new business deals were 24% larger, and win rates climbed more than 120% compared to deals without partners involved.

It takes a village—fortunately, you've already got one. Most companies have a well-established sales team before their partnership motion gets off the ground, and the beauty of the ecosystem-led sales playbook is how easily and powerfully it can be rolled out among an existing sales organization. From there, it creates outsized, measurable, repeatable results.

From start-ups to public juggernauts, we've seen the strategies in this chapter change the game for how modern companies go to market.

16

Ecosystem-Led Customer Success: Eliminate Churn and Grow Accounts

Perhaps the biggest slam-dunk in the account mapping matrix is the top-left corner, where your existing customers overlap with the customers of your partners (see Figure 16.1). Time and time again in this book, we've shown the data and stories of companies whose customers are more loyal and valuable when they are also deriving value from that company's ecosystem of partners.

This value can come in the form of technology integrations that combine to create new use cases or combined functionality. Or it can come in the form of service or agency relationships where a second party delivers implementations, services, or support to drive the success and adoption of a product.

Regardless of the nature of the partnership, there is an exceptionally powerful playbook that the best companies are running: increasing the joint value proposition offered when you and one or more partners have a joint customer. The ultimate outcome of all these plays is to use ELG to increase the **net revenue retention (NRR)** of your existing customer base.

NRR is driven by two main inputs: how many of your customers leave over time (**churn rate**) and how much more your existing customers pay you when they stay over long periods (expansion rate) (see Figure 16.2).

Benchmarks for best-in-class NRR are somewhat fluid based on your company's industry, billing model, and the state of the macro economy at any given time. During the market heyday of 2021, a desirable benchmark for NRR sat around 130%. In more challenging times, levels of 110%–120% are viewed as best-in-class.

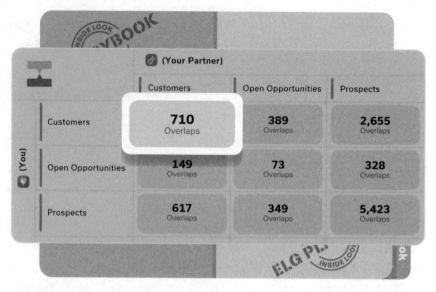

FIGURE 16.1 Account mapping matrix for overlapping customers.

$$\text{NRR} = \frac{(\,\text{Starting Revenue} + \text{Add-On Revenue}\,) - \text{Churned Revenue}}{\text{Starting Revenue}}$$

FIGURE 16.2 Net revenue retention (NRR) formula.

Regardless, the takeaway is clear: if you take a finite cohort of customers and see that you're losing more in **churn** than you're gaining in account expansion, you're in trouble. A sub-100% NRR company is often referred to as a "leaky bucket," and such companies are rarely able to reach escape velocity—the math is simply working too hard against them.

NRR is also a fantastic predictor of **customer lifetime value** (CLV, or CLTV), which is a key input to health metrics around economic efficiency, margin, and profitability. Healthy metrics across the board here are all on the critical path to building an enduring company.

So it should come as no surprise that ecosystem-led customer success, the practice of using ELG to reduce churn and expand accounts, is one of the hottest topics in the industry. The techniques in this section drive into how partner ecosystems can create a material impact on retention, expansion, and NRR.

Below we walk through the playbooks of companies that have driven NRR, retention, and churn reduction through ELG playbooks that enlist their technology and service partners.

Driving Customer Success with Tech Partners

In Crossbeam's 2023 State of the Partner Ecosystem report, we surveyed the data from hundreds of modern companies and collected a remarkable statistic: customers who take advantage of technology integrations into partner products are 58% less likely to churn on average.

Thanks to ELG data, there is a dead-simple calculation that you can do to track the success of every technology integration offered by your company. When you know the size of your overlapping customer base with a given partner, you know with high confidence the precise total serviceable market for an integration between your products.

Divide the number of customers actually using your integration with a partner by that overlapping customer count, and you'll know the precise market penetration of your integration, also known as its **adoption rate** (see Figure 16.3).

This is a gold mine. For one, the denominator of that formula alone can be one of the most powerful inputs to prioritizing which integrations to build in the first place. Understanding the "walk in" addressable market you'll have as soon as an integration goes live can help you rank prospective integrations quantitatively and make smarter decisions about where to invest time and resources.

You can even look at that data through the lens of total revenue, shared sales pipeline, or the profile of the overlapping companies to make more nuanced prioritization decisions based on the goals of your tech partnerships program. By picking the right bets, you can use your technology integrations as a change agent to enter new verticals, access new personas, or simply grow adoption and engagement in your existing base.

$$\textbf{ADOPTION RATE} = \frac{\textbf{Active Integration Users}}{\textbf{Total Overlapping Customers}}$$

FIGURE 16.3 Integration adoption math.

What's even more exciting is what comes next. Once an integration goes live, there exists a tried-and-true ELG playbook for driving widespread adoption of your new offering to the precise companies who can use it—without pestering the rest of your base or wasting precious customer attention span.

Natalie Fitzsimmons, senior partner marketing manager at RollWorks, knows this playbook inside and out. Rollworks, a division of NextRoll, offers ambitious B2B companies an account-based platform to align their marketing and sales teams and confidently grow revenue. When it comes to ecosystem-led customer success, RollWorks experiences the benefits firsthand:

- Customers who are using at least one partner integration renew at a roughly 30% higher rate than customers who don't.
- Rollworks customers using four or more integrations have a 135% likelihood to renew compared to customers using one integration.

"If your company can provide a much better customer experience, increase time to first value, and improve renewal rates by 30%, that should be a major input to your customer success strategy," says Fitzsimmons. Needless to say, Fitzsimmons and her team are heavily motivated to drive the adoption rate of their tech partner integrations.

When launching new integrations, the RollWorks partner marketing team runs targeted campaigns to reach precisely the addressable audience with precisely the right messaging. The secret sauce is an advertising campaign targeting mutual customers with programmatic digital ads. These campaigns are built by plugging ELG data about customer overlap directly into RollWorks's own platform. Fitzsimmons syncs partner overlap data from Crossbeam into RollWorks, making it easier to create dynamic, high-intent account lists and run partner-specific advertising campaigns.

These ads tease the core value proposition of using RollWorks and the partner's technology together and are served throughout each contact's web journey and on social media. They drive joint customers to simple, ungated eGuides that offer quick solutions to major pain points solved by the integration.

"We rely on dynamic lists from our ELG platform Crossbeam and the RollWorks integration to ensure our campaign messaging reaches the most relevant contacts ready to engage," says Fitzsimmons. "It's a foolproof way to unlock the value of shared partner data and has allowed us to collaborate with our partners in more meaningful and effective ways." The result: in one recent launch, they reached 68% integration adoption rate—exceeding their original goal to hit 50% adoption—in just 90 days.

This playbook has become a standard for all new integration launches at RollWorks. The RollWorks team plans to run similar campaigns in the near future not just to drive integration adoption among mutual customers but also to build partner-sourced sales pipeline by targeting prospects who are customers of partners.

Derek Safko at LeanData runs a complementary playbook that empowers his company's customer success team to drive adoption of their integrations—not just at launch, but continuously. LeanData's customer success managers (CSMs) are staying on top of integration adoption using the ELG reports and dashboards Safko has built in Salesforce. As new customers sign up for LeanData and CSMs are assigned those customers, their first move is to view the dashboard below to see which integration partners share that customer (see Figure 16.4).

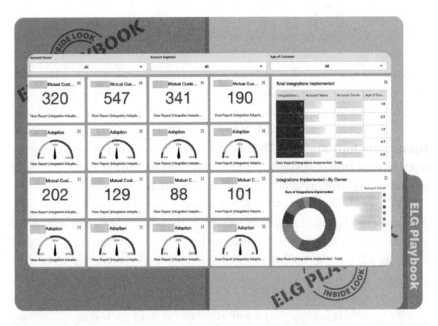

FIGURE 16.4 LeanData's CSM dashboard for integration adoption.

There are two ways LeanData's CSM might use this information to drive integration adoption:

1. If there is an upcoming meeting with the customer, the CSM can be prepared to discuss the integration, the benefits for the customer, and the steps to activate.
2. The CSM can proactively message the customer, either manually or through automated and personalized campaigns, to let them know about the integration and share collateral so the customer can learn more about the value of the integration and how to get started.

"Without insights into overlaps with our integration partners, it would be next to impossible to drive success around our integration adoption the way that we are today. ELG strategies powered by that data have changed everything," says Safko.

Driving Customer Success with Channel Partners

A company's value proposition is not wrapped up in its product alone. The ways in which that product is sold, implemented, serviced, enabled, trained, and grown are key parts of the customer experience. These factors can often have an outsized impact on customer loyalty and willingness to increase investment.

This is where channel partners—including system integrators, OEMs, agencies, and value-added resellers—come into play. No ecosystem-led customer success strategy is complete without an approach for involving and attaching such partners to customer relationships.

You may be familiar with Bombora. They invented "B2B intent data" and sell a product that helps companies understand when their customers and prospects are heavily increasing research on the products and services they sell.

Since the early 2020s, the team at Bombora has been on a mission to apply ELG practices that elevate the presence, influence, and impact of channel partners in how they sell and service accounts. And the results have been staggering.

"Creating loyal customers is a joint effort," says McKenzie Krizak, director of channel partnerships who began her career at Bombora in customer success. "Under this channel-focused strategy, our churn rate is 2.5x lower and our NPS scores have increased to over 70% being passive or promoter responses."

How did they do it? Like all great success stories, it started with a challenge.

"When sold directly, our customers in the midmarket were struggling to figure out how to use our data and get value out of their investment," says Krizak. "We were experiencing churn issues as a result and decided to take a new approach." That approach was to build a channel sales program for the mid-market that would allow Bombora data to be sold through channel partners rather than directly.

It's important to note that Bombora's channel program includes, and in fact primarily is driven through, its technology platform partners. More akin to a traditional OEM motion as described earlier in this book, a critical component of the Bombora channel turned out to be sell-through motions in which other platforms who leverage and activate Bombora data became the party primarily responsible for selling and servicing the accounts.

This hybrid tech/channel motion is an increasingly common addition to the channel strategy of modern companies, as the line between tech and channel partners blurs and the go-to-market capabilities of companies with tech-supported partnership continues to grow. However, the best practices shown here don't require a tech integration to work—the same playbooks can create powerful results with pure agency and service partners as well, of which Bombora also has a healthy ecosystem.

"Partnering with these channel sellers around very specific use cases started addressing the issues from our other sales motions where our customers were overwhelmed," said Brandon Balan, head of channel sales at Bombora. "What we learned is that customers who leveraged our data through this motion were a lot happier. They could activate it more easily, time to first value was significantly cut down, ROI was higher, and adoption across teams was also a lot higher."

With that data in hand, Bombora made the bold move of winding down its entire direct mid-market sales team and instead opted for a fully channel-driven sales motion for that market segment. Not only did this change drive the powerful results around customer success mentioned earlier, but Balan shared that it has also delivered a 3.5x higher close rate for new prospects who are channel-sourced and "in just sixteen months is well on the way to representing a third of the revenue that Bombora brings in."

Krizak shared the transformational impact this strategic shift has made in how Bombora approaches customer success. "Moving to this motion has taken a major weight off the shoulders of the post-sale team. It's no longer a solo effort, but instead you have multiple companies aligned around your customer's success."

Of course, this success isn't as simple as flipping a switch. Balan and Krizak share their playbook for a winning channel strategy, which cites four specific factors that have made their approach a winner:

A consultative approach to sales and service. We've all met salespeople who like to say that they are focused on creating value for customers, not selling (cue eye roll)—but at Bombora that's "actually a true thing," says Balan. "In most cases, we're not selling. We're helping. We are subject matter experts who become trusted advisors both with our partner sellers and with the client."

Balan shared that some of their reps are so deeply connected to their partners that they even have keycards that allow them to come and go to their offices. "Some have desks—one has a corner office!"

Ability to execute deals on partner paper. Bombora invested time and energy to allow their channel partners to function as resellers of their product. This reduces significant amounts of friction in the buying process because it meant new customers could simply buy Bombora's data as an add-on to an existing contract.

"We no longer have to deal with legal reviews, redlines, infosec reviews, and procurement people," said Balan. "All of that is gone by selling through these partners who have already gone through these processes."

Compensating partner reps for co-selling. "Most of our partners have moved to a place where their team—in both customer success and sales—are able to recognize the value of selling Bombora to their customer base. They're highly motivated," Balan told me.

Creating dedicated reps for each channel partner. Bombora reallocated some of our original mid-market team to dedicated reps who are focused on the success of specific channel partners. This helps them avoid conflict—per Balan, they can "remain Switzerland" even among partners who may compete with each other. "It also allows our reps to become experts on the partnership, knowing the ways in which each partner is the best at adding value."

The Bombora story is inspiring in many ways and shows the incredible superpowers that can be unlocked by building and unleashing a channel ecosystem to create happier and more loyal customers. The net effects on customer success and NRR are self-evident and undeniable in the hard data.

"The reason we're doing this is to continue to evolve and grow our business," Balan concludes. "By working with our channel partners, we've driven a better all-around experience that's leading to better deals, reduced churn, and set us up for long-term success."

Ecosystem-led customer success can sometimes feel like a freebie that comes automatically as a downstream effect of implementing ecosystem-led marketing and sales strategies. When customers come in with deep connections to the partner ecosystem, they can also unlock more value over time and with less friction—thus driving up NRR.

As we have seen, however, no one builds a world-class revenue organization by soaking the easy wins. There are important playbooks to put into motion at the customer success level that can turn ELG playbooks into NRR-driving machines. When it comes to growing accounts, the work is never truly done—but it can be automated, scaled, and measured.

In a world where profitability and efficiency continue to be scrutinized more than ever, doing the work to implement, scale, and sustain these ecosystem-led customer success strategies will only become more critical.

Conclusion: The Future of ELG

I wish I could have read this book back in my RJMetrics days. By the time I understood how partner ecosystems can shape billion-dollar companies, I had missed my first shot at creating one. Never again.

Today the world is different. Ecosystem-led growth has finally arrived, and this is just the beginning.

A few years back, Crossbeam began measuring a metric called the ELG index, which tracks the adoption of ecosystem-led growth among companies with partner ecosystems. In 2021, that number was so small that it was almost immeasurable. As of our first printing in 2024, it has risen to just over 6%.

I find this data noteworthy for two important reasons.

1. The growth of ELG adoption in the past few years has been extraordinary, showing an undeniable trend toward ELG practices becoming mainstream.
2. An adoption rate of 6% is still an incredibly small percentage, highlighting the huge magnitude of growth still ahead for this movement.

The shift toward ELG has now taken hold at thousands of companies, and as these playbooks continue to show traction across user personas, geographies, and industries, it will become nothing less than a full-on contagion.

Meanwhile, a powerful cocktail made up of nonzero interest rates, AI-powered innovators, and aggressive regulators is forcing companies to reassess (and often reject) just about every growth playbook that has worked over the past 20 years.

Unlike so many of these legacy playbooks, however, ELG is not a negative-sum game where early adopters benefit and the ROI thins out as it becomes more widely adopted.

To the contrary, ELG is positive-sum. Wider proliferation of ELG leads to denser, healthier ecosystems and shrinks the activation energy required for any company in those ecosystems to adopt it. Plus, it's proprietary, scalable, and efficient to boot.

Because ecosystems are a team sport, early adopters aren't just reaping powerful rewards—they're sharing the stories about how they did it. I'm profoundly grateful to the insightful leaders featured in this book from companies such as Stripe, Okta, Braze, Procore, Gong, Intercom, and Andreessen Horowitz. In the coming years, their ideas and experiences will propagate to countless other companies and allow the ELG index to rocket into the double digits on its path to 100%.

As ecosystem-led growth continues on this exciting trajectory, I hope the readers of this book feel better equipped to bring it to life inside their own companies and partner ecosystems. Regardless of what brought you here, I'm glad you made it to this page, and I thank you for your role in the exciting future ahead.

Glossary

Account Executive (AE)   A sales role typically responsible for closing deals with new customers.

Account Mapping   The process by which two or more partners compare lists of prospects, opportunities, or customers to identify overlapping relationships.

Account Mapping Matrix   A grid-like visual that summarizes the results of account mapping with a partner across multiple account lists. The most common account mapping matrix is a 3 × 3 grid that displays the size of the intersection between the lists of prospects, opportunities, and customers of two partners.

Account-Based Marketing (ABM)   A focused growth strategy in which marketing and sales teams collaborate to create personalized buying experiences for a specific set of high-value accounts. Rather than casting a wide net with their marketing efforts, businesses identify key potential or existing customers (accounts) and tailor customized strategies and messages to them.

Agency Partner   An organization or individual that collaborates with companies to manage marketing campaigns or implement products on behalf of their mutual clients. Agency partners often bring specialized expertise or resources to the table, allowing businesses to extend their reach, improve the quality of their service, or tap into new markets.

Annual Contract Value (ACV)   The value of a specific customer's contract or subscription with your company on an annual basis. (Confusingly, it shares its acronym with average contract value.)

Application Programming Interface (API)   A set of protocols and tools that allow different software applications to communicate and interact with each other.

Attribution   The process of measuring and assigning credit to various actions, activities, or channels that contribute to a desired outcome, such as closing a deal.

Audit Logs   Records that capture and document actions taken, including changes and configurations.

Average Contract Value (ACV)   The average size of the annual contract value across your customer base or a specific subset of customers. (Confusingly, it shares its acronym with annual contract value.)

Business Development Representative (BDR)   An alternative title for a sales development representative (SDR), sometimes used when that person does not report into a sales team or for the optics of not appearing "salesy" when doing outreach.

Business Intelligence Software   Tools and technologies that help businesses collect, process, and analyze data to make informed decisions.

California Consumer Privacy Act (CCPA)   A California state law enacted in 2018 that grants consumers increased control over their personal data. It gives residents of California the right to know what personal information businesses collect about them, the purpose of collection, and if that information is sold or shared with third parties. It also provides consumers the right to opt out of the sale of their personal data and the right to request the deletion of their information.

Capital Efficiency   The extent to which a business is able to generate desirable financial outputs (such as revenue or profit) with minimal levels of investment. This efficiency can apply to the overall finances of a company or specifically to the cost profile of driving incremental growth.

Channel Partnerships   Partnerships through which companies leverage distribution channels, such as resellers or distributors, to expand their market reach or improve their value proposition. Channel partners are incentivized by referral fees or by the sale of complementary services, including consulting, training, and customer support.

ChatGPT   A large language model (LLM) developed by OpenAI, designed to produce coherent and contextually relevant text based on user prompts. It facilitates humanlike interactions, making it useful for conversations, content creation, and a range of other applications.

Churn   The phenomenon of customers discontinuing their use of or subscription to a company's product or service over a given time period.

Churn Rate   A percentage representing the ratio of the number of customers or subscription dollars a company has lost to the starting amount for that period. High churn rates can signal customer dissatisfaction, and reducing churn is crucial for business growth and maintaining revenue streams.

Cold Start Problem   A predicament often faced when initiating new networks or platforms, where the inherent value of the network remains uncertain until it reaches a certain size or level of engagement. It's akin to the chicken-and-egg dilemma: for the network to be valuable, it needs users, but to attract users, it needs to demonstrate its value.

Co-Marketing   A collaborative marketing strategy wherein partnership teams from different organizations join forces to promote products, services, or content to specific audiences or market segments.

Co-Selling   A collaborative sales strategy wherein two or more partner organizations jointly engage in the sales process. By pooling resources, expertise, and solutions, they can more effectively generate leads, convert prospects, and expand existing accounts. It is a cornerstone playbook of ecosystem-led sales.

Comma-Separated Values (CSV)   A widely used file format for storing and exchanging data. In a CSV file, each line represents a data record, with individual fields (or values) separated by commas. Due to its simplicity and broad application in data processing tools, spreadsheets, and databases, CSV is a popular choice for data import/export.

Content Marketing   A strategic approach within inbound marketing where businesses produce and share valuable, relevant, and consistent content to attract and retain a defined audience. By offering educational and engaging material, companies aim to establish themselves as thought leaders, foster trust, and ultimately drive customer action.

Conversion Rate   The percentage of prospects or leads who take a desired action, such as making a purchase, signing up for a newsletter, or filling out a contact form. In B2B sales, it often refers to the proportion of sales opportunities who become paying customers.

Crossbeam   The world's first and largest ELG platform, used by over 15,000 companies to enable, execute, and measure the success of their ELG playbooks.

Customer Lifetime Value (CLV or CLTV)   The predicted net profit attributed to the entire future relationship with a customer.

Customer Relationship Management (CRM)   A system or software designed to manage a company's interactions with current and potential customers. It centralizes, organizes, and tracks customer information, sales opportunities, communications, and other touchpoints, facilitating better decision-making, improved customer service, and strengthened relationships.

Customer Success Manager (CSM) A professional role dedicated to proactively guiding and supporting customers in their journey with a company's products or services. CSMs ensure customers derive maximum value, leading to higher satisfaction, engagement, and retention. Their focus is not just on resolving issues but on anticipating needs, fostering relationships, and helping customers achieve their desired outcomes.

Data Broker A company that collects and sells data about individuals and businesses.

Data Fields Individual pieces of information stored in a dataset, such as company name, website URL, or other attributes.

Data Mapping The process of associating data from one source to corresponding data in another source.

Data-Sharing Rules Guidelines that dictate what data is shared with partners and under what circumstances.

Data Silos Isolated collections of data within a company or between companies that hinder the sharing and collaboration of information due to technical or compliance constraints.

Data Warehouse A centralized repository for storing, organizing, and analyzing large volumes of data.

Deal Stage The specific phase in the sales process that a deal or opportunity is currently in.

Distributor A channel partner that typically does not sell directly to end users. Instead, they sit in the middle between manufacturers and other resellers or retailers who interface with the end consumer of the product.

Ecosystem Often used as shorthand for "partner ecosystem," it refers to the interconnected network of businesses, solutions, and services that coexist and collaborate within a specific industry or around a technology platform.

Ecosystem-Led Customer Success The practice of using ecosystem-led growth playbooks to retain and expand the revenue of existing customer accounts.

Ecosystem-Led Growth (ELG) A go-to-market motion that focuses on the partner ecosystem as the primary way to attract, convert, and grow customer relationships.

Ecosystem-Led Marketing The practice of using ecosystem-led growth playbooks to drive a steady flow of qualified, efficient pipeline to the top of your revenue funnel.

Ecosystem-Led Sales The practice of using ecosystem-led growth playbooks to convert sales opportunities into paying customers.

Ecosystem Qualified Lead (EQL) A prospective customer or sales opportunity identified through ecosystem-led growth strategies. Unlike traditional leads, EQLs are primarily qualified based on their established connections within a company's partner ecosystem. These connections are leveraged to drive sales opportunities, as they often signal a higher propensity for engagement or conversion due to the inherent trust and mutual benefits within the ecosystem.

ELG Index An industry measurement conducted by Crossbeam that reflects the rate of adoption of ELG among companies with partner ecosystems.

ELG Platform A software product that directly enables ecosystem-led growth practices by hosting a network of connected companies, facilitates controlled data sharing, and provides workflows for executing on ELG playbooks.

Extract, Load, Transform (ELT) An approach in data processing where data is first extracted from source systems and then loaded directly into a destination database or data warehouse. Only after this is the data transformed, typically using the processing power of the database or data warehouse itself. This contrasts with the traditional ETL method, where data is transformed before loading.

Extract, Transform, Load (ETL) An approach in data processing where data is first extracted from heterogeneous source systems (such as databases, CRM systems, or flat files). It is then transformed into a consistent, clean, and usable format, often involving operations such as cleansing, aggregating, enriching, and reformatting. Finally, the transformed data is loaded into a target database, typically a data warehouse, for analytics and reporting purposes.

Expansion Rate The rate at which current customers expand their spending with a company, often through upsells, cross-sells, or increased usage.

General Data Protection Regulation (GDPR) A comprehensive regulation introduced by the European Union in 2018, aimed at ensuring the protection of individuals' personal data and privacy rights. It mandates transparency from organizations about how they collect, use, and store personal data.

Generative AI   Artificial intelligence systems capable of creating new content, be it text, images, or even code. Trained on vast datasets using machine learning algorithms, these systems can autonomously generate content that's often indistinguishable from what humans produce.

Global System Integrators (GSIs)   Large multinational firms that specialize in bringing together various technologies to design and deliver comprehensive IT solutions. They operate across multiple industries and regions, often partnering with technology vendors to cater to the needs of global clients.

Gross Domestic Product (GDP)   The total monetary value of all goods and services produced within a country's borders in a specific time period.

Hyperscalers   Large tech companies, such as Amazon, Google, and Microsoft, that have vast infrastructure capacities and scale their resources aggressively. They aim not only to dominate the public cloud market but also to influence the broader digital ecosystems and economies stemming from their platforms.

Inbound Marketing   A marketing strategy that centers on drawing customers to a business organically. This is achieved by producing valuable content, optimizing for search engines (SEO), engaging on social media, and other methods that naturally lead potential customers to the company's digital presence.

Independent Software Vendor (ISV)   Firms that create software products intended for integration or use with other companies' platforms or technologies. These products can either be stand-alone applications or enhancements to existing systems.

Industry Alliances   Collaborative groupings, often akin to trade associations, where member companies come together to share knowledge, resources, and strategies specific to their industry.

Integration   A process or software solution that enables two or more distinct software applications or platforms to connect and exchange data seamlessly, creating a more streamlined customer experience and new joint value proposition across products.

ISO Certification   The ISO/IEC 27001 certification is an internationally recognized benchmark for information security management. Achieving this certification indicates a company's commitment to adhering to rigorous information security controls via its information security management system (ISMS) and internal processes. The ISO/IEC 27701, a subsequent certification focused on data privacy, builds on the principles of ISO/IEC 27001. To be eligible for ISO/IEC 27701, companies must first achieve the ISO/IEC 27001 certification.

J-Curve   A graphical representation of the initial negative impact (investment) followed by positive returns over time, forming a curve that resembles the letter "J."

Key Performance Indicator (KPI)   A measurable value that indicates how effectively a company is achieving its key business objectives. KPIs are used to evaluate success at reaching targets across various aspects of performance, from financial achievements to marketing and operational goals.

Large Language Model (LLM)   A subset of generative AI models, LLMs are specifically tailored to understand and produce humanlike language. These models, such as ChatGPT and GPT-4, undergo training on enormous text datasets, enabling them to generate coherent and contextually appropriate text responses.

Managed Service Provider (MSP)   A firm that delivers a range of IT services, either remotely or on-site. MSPs manage, monitor, and maintain a client's technology infrastructure, ensuring seamless IT operations and often providing a subscription-based model for their services.

Marketplace   Within modern digital ecosystems, a marketplace is an online platform or portal where products or services are transacted. Acting as a trusted intermediary, the marketplace facilitates exchanges, often removing the need for direct contracts between buyers and sellers. Notable examples in the tech domain include the marketplaces provided by hyperscalers such as Amazon Web Services (AWS), Google Cloud Platform (GCP), and Microsoft Azure.

Nash Equilibrium   A concept in game theory in which each player's strategy is optimal given the strategies chosen by the other players. In this state, no player has an incentive to unilaterally change their strategy, as doing so wouldn't lead to a better outcome.

Net Revenue Retention (NRR)   A metric used to measure the percentage change in revenue from existing customers over a given period. It takes into account revenue gains from upsells or expansions and subtracts losses from downgrades, contractions, and churn. A value greater than 100% indicates net growth, while a value less than 100% indicates net revenue loss from the existing customer base.

Opportunity A potential sale or deal that has been identified and is actively being pursued by a sales team. In CRM systems and sales pipelines, opportunities represent leads or accounts that have reached a stage where there's a likelihood of closing a sale.

Organic A descriptor assigned to inbound website traffic, leads, opportunities, or customers who were acquired without the use of paid acquisition channels or other expenditures.

Original Equipment Manufacturer (OEM) A type of partnership wherein one company integrates another company's product or component into its own product, often rebranding or co-branding it.

Partner An outside company, organization, or person with whom you "win together."

Partner Ecosystem An interconnected network of businesses, communities, and individuals that work together and often rely on each other to offer end-to-end value to their shared customers or prospects.

Partner Ecosystem Platform (PEP) A rarely used legacy term for a class of software companies who aid in powering ecosystem-led growth strategies. Such companies are now more commonly referred to as ELG platforms.

Partner Relationship Management (PRM) A specialized platform designed to enable companies to effectively manage and collaborate with their partners. PRMs streamline various aspects of partner management including training, documentation distribution, lead registration, and commission management.

Partner Influenced A label denoting that a partner's actions, strategies, or behaviors contributed, either directly or indirectly, to a specific positive outcome. This influence can coexist with other contributing factors.

Partner Sourced Indicates that a specific lead, opportunity, or customer was directly acquired or originated due to a partner's initiatives. As this descriptor signifies the partner's primary and exclusive role in sourcing, it is often viewed as more significant than mere partner influence.

Penetration Tests In-depth security assessments carried out by specialized firms or professionals to detect and analyze vulnerabilities in a system or network. The goal is to identify potential security flaws before malicious actors can exploit them.

Personally Identifiable Information (PII) Any data that can be used to identify a specific individual, either alone or in combination with other information. Examples include names, addresses, phone numbers, and

Social Security numbers. Safeguarding PII is critical for businesses, as mishandling it can lead to privacy breaches and legal consequences.

Populations   Also called "account segments," "account lists," or "match lists," these are lists of people or companies that are categorized based on certain attributes. They are typically the raw inputs to an account mapping process and used to find overlaps between partners' data via ELG platforms. Common populations include prospects, opportunities, and customers.

Power Law Curve   A statistical phenomenon where a limited number of events or participants yield the majority of the results.

Prisoner's Dilemma   A foundational scenario in game theory illustrating the conflict between individual and collective rationality. Participants often end up with suboptimal results due to mistrust and a lack of collaboration, even when cooperation would yield a more favorable outcome for both.

Procurement Process   The method followed by businesses to acquire goods and services. It encompasses a sequence of activities, from identifying needs, sourcing suppliers, negotiating terms, and finalizing the purchase.

Product-Led Growth (PLG)   A business growth strategy powered by a product's inherent value and ability to attract, convert, and retain customers. PLG aims to organically draw and retain users, minimizing acquisition costs and spurring growth via positive feedback and referrals.

Product-Market Fit (PMF)   The juncture at which a product's capabilities align seamlessly with the demands and requirements of its intended market, signaling its readiness for broader market deployment.

Product-Qualified Lead (PQL)   A potential customer that has shown notable engagement with a product, typically through trials, demos, or usage metrics, suggesting an increased likelihood of conversion.

Prospect   A potential customer that a business has identified as fitting their target profile but hasn't yet transitioned into an active opportunity or paying client.

Public Cloud   Services provided by cloud computing companies that are available to the public on a subscription or pay-as-you-go basis. While Amazon Web Services, Google Cloud Platform, and Microsoft Azure are leading providers, the term can encompass a range of other providers offering similar services.

Regional System Integrators (RSIs) System integrators specializing in serving specific regions or niches. Their localized focus allows for tailored solutions in accordance with regional or industry-specific needs.

Reseller Partners Business entities that purchase products or services from primary vendors to sell them to end consumers. This can further extend to value-added resellers (VARs), who not only resell products but also offer additional services or enhancements, ranging from product integration, consulting, and training to other complementary services.

Return on Investment (ROI) A financial metric used to evaluate the efficiency and profitability of an investment. Typically calculated by comparing the net profit of an investment to its initial cost, it provides insight into the value derived from a particular investment relative to its cost.

Sales Development Representatives (SDRs) Team members specifically tasked with identifying and qualifying potential customers (leads) for the sales team. They initiate the sales process by generating interest and scheduling meetings. While SDR is the most common term, roles with similar responsibilities may also be referred to as BDRs (business development representatives) or ADRs (account development representatives).

Sales Engagement Platform A platform that helps sales teams manage, automate, and optimize their interactions with leads and prospects.

Sales-Led Growth (SLG) A growth strategy that relies heavily on sales teams and traditional sales processes to drive revenue and customer acquisition.

Sales Pipeline A company's current total universe of prospective customers, often limited to those qualified and likely to purchase within a finite time horizon.

Search Engine Optimization (SEO) The process of enhancing a website's visibility in search engine results through optimization of its content, structure, and other elements.

Second-Party Data Data generated by one organization and then shared, often through direct partnerships or collaborations, with another organization. This data contrasts with first-party data, which is sourced directly from an organization's own interactions with customers or users, and third-party data, which is sourced from marketplaces or data brokers who have no direct relationship to the data's end user.

Serviceable Obtainable Market (SOM) A segment of the total addressable market (TAM) that can be realistically captured and served by a company, considering its current resources, capabilities, and competition.

Single Sign-On (SSO) A user authentication process that permits an individual to enter one set of credentials (such as a username and password) to access multiple applications. For businesses, SSO enhances security by centralizing the authentication process, reducing the risk of password-related breaches and simplifying password management.

SOC 2 An audit framework developed by the American Institute of Certified Public Accountants (AICPA). It evaluates and reports on the effectiveness of an organization's reporting controls as they relate to security, availability, processing integrity, confidentiality, and privacy of a system. SOC 2 Type I reports evaluate the design of controls at a specific point in time, while SOC 2 Type II reports evaluate the design and operating effectiveness of controls over a specified review period.

Software as a Service (SaaS) A cloud-based software distribution model where applications are hosted by a third-party provider. Instead of purchasing and installing software locally, users can access the application and its features over the Internet, typically on a subscription basis.

Stakeholders Individuals, groups, or entities that have a vested interest in the outcome of a project, decision, or business activity. Stakeholders can influence or be influenced by the organization's actions, objectives, and policies.

"State of the Partner Ecosystem" (SOPE) An in-depth annual survey conducted by Crossbeam. The SOPE report sheds light on the prevailing trends, challenges, and sentiments within the partnership ecosystem, offering valuable insights for industry professionals.

Strategic Partnerships Formalized collaborations between two or more companies aiming for mutual benefit. Unlike acquisitions or joint ventures where companies merge or pool resources, strategic partnerships involve cooperation while retaining their separate identities. These partnerships often pave the way for deeper integrations and in some cases, acquisitions.

System Integrators (SIs) Companies or consultants specializing in bringing together various technological components into a cohesive system. They assess a client's existing tech infrastructure, suggest improvements, and oversee the implementation of those changes. Their expertise ensures that various components, software, and processes work seamlessly together.

Technology Partnership   A collaboration between two or more companies where they integrate their respective technologies or products. By combining their strengths and capabilities, tech partners can create improved workflows, exchange valuable data, trigger events, and develop shared go-to-market strategies.

The Partnership Paradox   A common phenomenon in which there is a profound discrepancy between the self-perceived value of a partnership department and the resources allocated to them.

Total Addressable Market (TAM)   The entire revenue opportunity that exists for a particular product or service. It provides an upper limit on potential sales and serves as a reference point for companies looking to evaluate the potential scale of their endeavors.

Value-Added Reseller (VAR)   A business entity that collaborates with partners to further develop or modify a product, adding distinctive features or functionalities before reselling it.

White Labeling   This process involves one company using another's product or service but branding and presenting it as if it were their own. It allows companies to expand their product or service offerings without having to develop new solutions from scratch.

Zero Interest Rate Phenomenon (ZIRP)   Companies or investments that primarily thrive or even solely exist because of the excessive capital funneled into them in an environment characterized by low interest rates. The phenomenon suggests that once interest rates rise or the capital climate tightens, these entities might struggle to sustain themselves.

Bibliography

"Accenture 2020 Earnings Reports." Accenture, 2020. https://investor.accenture.com/filings-and-reports/earnings-reports/2020.

"Account Mapping Matrix in Crossbeam." Crossbeam, August 2, 2023. https://app.crossbeam.com/.

"Adobe and Microsoft Expand Partnership with Adobe Experience Manager and Dynamics 365 Integration." TechCrunch, November 7, 2017. https://techcrunch.com/2017/11/03/adobe-and-microsoft-expand-partnership-with-adobe-experience-manager-and-dynamics-365-integration/.

"Amazon Redshift Announcement Release." AWS, November 28, 2012. https://aws.amazon.com/about-aws/whats-new/2012/11/28/announcing-amazon-redshift/.

Andreessen, Marc. "Why Software Is Eating the World." Andreessen Horowitz, August 20, 2011. https://a16z.com/2011/08/20/why-software-is-eating-the-world/.

"Apple and Salesforce Bring Together the Best Devices for Business and the World's #1 CRM." Apple, September 24, 2018. https://www.apple.com/newsroom/2018/09/apple-and-salesforce-partner-to-help-redefine-customer-experiences-on-ios/.

"Atlassian + Slack." Slack, July 26, 2018. https://slack.com/blog/news/atlassian-and-slack-partnership.

"Average Sales Development Representative Salary in U.S." Glassdoor, August 29, 2023. https://www.glassdoor.com/Salaries/us-sales-development-representative-salary-SRCH_IL.0,2_IN1_KO3,35.htm?clickSource=searchBtn.

B&W Photograph Generated by the Author via Midjourney. AI Photograph. Midjourney, August 11, 2023.

"CDW 2020 Annual Report." CDW, 2021. https://s23.q4cdn.com/113947819/files/doc_financials/2020/ar/CDW-2020-Annual-Report-Form-10K.pdf.

Chen, Andrew. The Cold Start Problem: Using Network Effects to Scale Your Product. New York: Random House, 2021.

"Clari Homepage, April 2023." Clari, April 1, 2023. https://www.clari.com/.

Clarke, Gavin. "The Register Headline: Redshift Is Fastest Growing AWS Service Ever, Says Amazon." The Register, April 15, 2015. https://www.theregister.com/2015/04/15/amazon_redshift_big_growth/.

"Data Warehouse Showdown: Redshift vs. Postgres." Sisense, 2015. https://www.sisense.com/blog/redshift-and-rds-postgres-benchmarked/.

"dbt Labs Raises $222M in Series D Funding at $4.2B Valuation Led by Altimeter with Participation from Databricks and Snowflake." *PR Newswire*, February 24, 2022. https://www.prnewswire.com/news-releases/dbt-labs-raises-222m-in-series-d-funding-at-4-2b-valuation-led-by-altimeter-with-participation-from-databricks-and-snowflake-301489733.html.

"DiscoverOrg Homepage, March 2013." DiscoverOrg, March 15, 2013. https://discoverorg.com/.

"DocuSign in Salesforce." DocuSign, August 31, 2023. https://www.docusign.com/integrations/salesforce.

"Embedded Analytics Tools & Software." Sigma, August 28, 2023. https://www.sigmacomputing.com/product/embedded-analytics.

Fox, Justin. "How to Succeed in Business by Bundling—and Unbundling." *Harvard Business Review*, June 24, 2014. https://hbr.org/2014/06/how-to-succeed-in-business-by-bundling-and-unbundling.

"Get Your Sales Team Excited About Co-Selling with a 50% Faster Time to Close." Crossbeam, December 3, 2020. https://insider.crossbeam.com/resources/freshworks-rajiv-ramanan-coselling-partner-influenced-deals.

"Gong Homepage, April 2023." Gong, April 1, 2023. https://www.gong.io/.

"Google Cloud and VMware Expand Global Partnership to Help Enterprises Accelerate App Modernization and Cloud Transformation." *Vmware*, March 16, 2022. https://news.vmware.com/releases/vmware-google-cloud-expanded-partnership.

"How Bombora Discovered Hidden Pipeline and Closed $100K in 2 Months with Crossbeam." Crossbeam, August 31, 2023. https://www.crossbeam.com/resources/case-studies/how-bombora-discovered-hidden-pipeline-and-closed-100k-in-2-months-with-crossbeam/.

"How Everflow Used Partner Data to Shave Four Months Off of Enterprise Deal Cycles." Crossbeam, August 31, 2023. https://www.crossbeam.com/resources/case-studies/how-everflow-shaved-four-months-off-of-enterprise-deal-cycles-with-partner-data/

"How Hatch Boosted Its Close Rate by 24% by Incentivizing its Partner's Account Managers." Crossbeam, July 29, 2021. https://insider.crossbeam.com/resources/hatch-closing-deals-faster-incentivizing-partners-account-managers.

"How LeanData Makes It Easy for Reps to Close Partner-Sourced Revenue." Crossbeam, August 31, 2023. https://www.crossbeam.com/resources/case-studies/how-leandata-makes-it-easy-for-reps-to-close-partner-sourced-revenue/.

"How Okta Ventures Surfaced 60 Ecosystem Qualified Leads for Its Portfolio Companies in Just Two Weeks." Crossbeam, August 31, 2023. https://www.crossbeam.com/resources/case-studies/how-okta-ventures-surfaced-60-ecosystem-qualified-leads-for-its-portfolio-companies-in-just-two-weeks/.

"How RingCentral Built an Internal Culture of Partnerships." Crossbeam, April 28, 2022. https://insider.crossbeam.com/resources/how-ringcentral-built-internal-culture-of-partnerships.

"HubSpot Founder on Building a $20B Business." *The Logan Bartlett Show*, March 24, 2023. Video. https://www.youtube.com/watch?v=eO9asQJXoeU.

"The Importance of Partnerships in the Great Unbundling." *a16z Live*, June 30, 2022. https://a16z.com/2022/06/30/the-importance-of-partnerships-in-the-great-unbundling/.

"Insight Enterprises, Inc. Reports Fourth Quarter and Record Results for the Full Year 2020." Insight Enterprises, February 11, 2021. https://investor.insight.com/news-releases/news-release-details/2021/Insight-Enterprises-Inc.-Reports-Fourth-Quarter-and-Record-Results-for-the-Full-Year-2020/.

"Intercom's Playbook for Ecosystem-Led Growth (+ 30% More Sourced Revenue)." Crossbeam, August 31, 2023. https://www.crossbeam.com/resources/case-studies/intercoms-playbook-for-ecosystem-led-growth/.

"Invictus Growth Partners Invests $43 Million in Software Maker Allbound." *Wall Street Journal*, July 26, 2022. https://www.wsj.com/articles/invictus-growth-partners-invests-43-million-in-software-maker-allbound-11658831401.

"iOS 14 Opt-in Rate—Weekly Updates Since Launch" Flurry. May 25, 2021. https://www.flurry.com/blog/ios-14-5-opt-in-rate-idfa-app-tracking-transparency-weekly/.

"ISO/IEC 27001 Certification." Crossbeam, August 2, 2023. https://www.crossbeam.com/how-it-works/security/.

"ISO/IEC 27701 Privacy Certification." Crossbeam, August 2, 2023. https://www.crossbeam.com/how-it-works/security/.

Kelly, Zoë. "Partnerships 101: What Is Partner Marketing." *Crossbeam Insider*, May 6, 2022. https://insider.crossbeam.com/resources/partnerships-101-what-is-partner-marketing.

"LeanData's ELG Dashboard View (Data Redacted)." LeanData, April 28, 2023. https://www.leandata.com/.

"Mapping ELG Plays via the Account Mapping Matrix." Crossbeam, August 2, 2023. https://app.crossbeam.com/.

"Meta's Ad Practices Ruled Illegal under GDPR: Key Facts and Implications of the Decision." Piwik PRO, February 1, 2023. https://piwik.pro/blog/metas-ad-practices-ruled-illegal/.

Moore, Robert. *Data Warehousing*. Graphic. RJMetrics, January 1, 2011.

Moore, Robert. *Pam and Bob at the Supernode 2023 Conference*. 2023. Photograph. August 31, 2023.

Moore, Robert. "RJMetrics Acquired by Magento Commerce, Pipeline Is Now Stitch." RJMetrics, August 1, 2016. https://blog.rjmetrics.com/2016/08/01/rjmetrics-acquired-by-magento-commerce-pipeline-is-now-stitch/.

Moore, Robert. "RJMetrics Revenue and Customer Growth: The Bootstrap Years." Graphic. RJMetrics, November 1, 2013.

Moore, Robert. "When We Lost the Warehouse, We Lost Our Way." Graphic. RJMetrics, 2011.

"Partner Attribution Tagging in Crossbeam." Crossbeam, August 2, 2023. https://app.crossbeam.com/.

"Partnerships 101: Sandboxes (And Why You Should Consider Building One)." Crossbeam, August 12, 2022. https://insider.crossbeam.com/resources/partnerships-101-sandboxes-and-why-you-should-consider-building-one.

"Partnerships for the Win: How Census Uses Partner Data to Pursue Higher ACVs." Crossbeam, August 31, 2023. https://www.crossbeam.com/resources/case-studies/how-census-uses-partner-data-to-pursue-higher-acvs/.

"PLG & Profitability: More Product Doesn't Necessarily Mean Greater Profits." Tomasz Tunguz, December 7, 2022. https://tomtunguz.com/plg-less-profitable/.

"Reporting Analytics Reporting Tools & Software." Sigma Computing, August 31, 2023. https://www.sigmacomputing.com/product/embedded-analytics.

"RollWorks Embraced the Partner Cloud. Now, They Have a 30% Increase in Retention." Crossbeam, August 31, 2023. https://www.crossbeam.com/resources/case-studies/rollworks-embraced-the-partner-cloud-crossbeam/.

Ross, Aaron, and Marylou Tyler. *Predictable Revenue*. West Hollywood: PebbleStorm, 2011.

"SDR View of Ecosystem Overlaps in Salesforce." Crossbeam, August 2, 2023. https://app.crossbeam.com/.

"SHI International Earns Record $12.3 Billion in 2021 Revenue, Up 10% Year Over Year." SHI International, March 7, 2022. https://www.shi.com/about/news/shi-revenue-second-half-2021.

Sisense. "SiSense Benchmarking Study Outputs," 2015.

"Snowflake's High-Density Partner Ecosystem via Partnerbase.Com." Partnerbase, April 28, 2023. https://partnerbase.com/snowflake.

"SOC 2 Type II Compliance." Crossbeam, August 2, 2023. https://www.crossbeam.com/how-it-works/security/.

"State of Sales Development 2022." Pavilion, October 24, 2022. https://www.joinpavilion.com/resource/state-of-sales-development-2022.

"State of the Partner Ecosystem 2023." Crossbeam, February 14, 2023. https://www.crossbeam.com/resources/webinars/the-state-of-the-partner-ecosystem-2023/.

"The Crossbeam Salesforce Widget (Simulated Data)." Crossbeam, August 2, 2023. https://app.crossbeam.com/.

"The Data Sync Selection Tool in Crossbeam." Crossbeam, August 2, 2023. https://app.crossbeam.com/.

Umbach, Valentin. "The Modern Data Stack Map by Valentin Umbach" (@Valentin-Umbach on X). Graphic. July 22, 2021. https://twitter.com/ValentinUmbach/status/1418242294952644611.

"Who Is Zift." ZoomInfo, August 28, 2023. https://www.zoominfo.com/c/zift-llc/398055050.

"Who Is Zinfi Technologies." ZoomInfo, August 28, 2023. https://www.zoominfo.com/c/zinfi-technologies-inc/100581378.

"Why Ecosystem-Led Marketing Rules: How to Get 60% Higher Engagement Rates On Your Next Integration Adoption Campaign" Crossbeam. August 31, 2023. https://www.crossbeam.com/resources/case-studies/why-elm-rules-how-to-get-60-higher-engagement-integration-adoption/.

"ZoomInfo Homepage, April 2023." ZoomInfo, April 1, 2023. https://www.zoominfo.com/.

Author Bio

Bob Moore is cofounder and CEO of Crossbeam, an ecosystem-led growth (ELG) platform that helps companies use their partner ecosystems to generate leads, close deals, and grow faster.

Moore previously cofounded the cloud data pipeline company Stitch (acquired by Talend in 2018) and business intelligence platform RJMetrics (acquired by Adobe by way of Magento Commerce in 2016).

Prior to RJMetrics, Moore worked on the Investment Team of Insight Partners, a leading software-focused venture capital and private equity firm based in New York. He is a graduate of Princeton University's School of Engineering and Applied Science.

Bob is a proud Philadelphian, where he serves as a trustee of the Franklin Institute, one of the oldest and premier centers of science education and development in the country. He has also previously served as the board chair of the Philly Startup Leaders and as a board member of the Philadelphia Alliance for Capital and Technologies (PACT).

As a writer and speaker, Bob's work has appeared in the *New York Times*, *Forbes*, TechCrunch, VentureBeat, Web Summit, TEDx, and Business of Software, among many others. He guest-lectures regularly at Princeton University and the Wharton School.

Outside of work, Bob is an improv comedy performer, where he most notably has performed over 100 shows as a member of the improv team Big Baby and is a multi-time winner of "Eat Your Beets," a freestyle comedy rap competition.

He lives in New Jersey with his wife and two daughters, who thankfully aren't yet old enough to be embarrassed by any of this.

Index